Another Farewell to the Theatre

UPCOMING BOOKS FROM THE LICHTENBERGIAN PRESS

The Buttocks Thing | W. Jeff Bishop

Bear & Rabbit | W. Jeff Bishop

Imprisonment: finding the way | Craig Humphrey

A Perfect Life | Dale Lyles

Lichtenbergianism: procrastination as a creative strategy | Dale Lyles

Another Farewell to the Theatre

Occasional Writings,
2000-2013
Marc Honea

published by

The Lichtenbergian Press

CATALOGING IN PUBLICATION
Honea, Marc 1962–
Another farewell to the theatre / Marc Honea
1. Theater Apologetic Works. 2. Theater Study and teaching. 3. Vocal
Sequence (Herbert Blau and Kraken) 4. Psychoanalysis, Jacques Lacan,
sinthome. I. Title
PN2035
792.028

Book design by Dale Lyles
Fonts used: text, Minion Pro; headings, AlexandraFLF; aphorisms, Avenir Next; haiku, Gill Sans

for JP:

How all occasions do inform against me...

Contents

Introduction

Whatever you're looking for, you won't find it here.

As mottos go, not too promising. Not at all promising, in fact. And yet. Can't we agree that something is there? Once we've reached the end and look back? Back to the pause, the comma? Something is there, but it's not articulated. Something is implied. Something positive within the negative. Irony, right? That's the term. It's there haunting and hovering, but it's not scripted. Certainly, that, in a nutshell, is a statement of an aesthetic. And it's safe, seemingly. There be no dragons there or work making anyone free. No false promises, thankfully, but no abandoning of hope, either; good news for those who might dare to enter and check things out. We also note with relief that the exits are lighted.

I like this motto. I just thought of it, but I find it easy to believe that it has always been there. Framed. On the wall. Or above the door. To my mind it testifies (along with those marked exits) to the fact that we are in a theatre. I can imagine a cadre of eager archeologists finding a sign buried in the rubble. It is the few faint traces of this motto remaining on the bit of dried board that tells them they are standing amidst the ruins of a theatre. It's that kind of incontrovertible inscription. Or, to conceive a scenario closer to our own time, perhaps a few of us found a way to escape before the town's ghosting implosion. We made it out alive but now have returned seeking the warm glow of nostalgia and a bit of closure. As we move about the space wrapped in a full and choking silence, one of us finds the sign. We wipe away the dust and smile at our motto. We remember the work that took place in the space, if this was the space—there were actually a number of spaces—and we remember the hope for an understanding audience. There was that one time, *wasn't there*?

With a motto, I can close an era. The first decade of our new century. Done. I lock up and give the sign a nudge. It gently rocks. The motto allows me to write the ending. Memory is now *era-gated*. Closed and full. Perhaps there can be some form of harvest.

Time for a confession. The motto is mine, but it's also borrowed. It's pulled from Jacques Lacan. I changed it a bit to serve my own ends, but I can't escape the original resonance.

In truth, this collection of writings is documentation of my struggle with my Lacan heritage, with the fact that I can't just quell the echoes. I devoted a good bit of time and effort to studying Lacan (yes, I know—for good or ill!). After an earlier "Farewell to the Theatre" from a previous decade, I spent a number of years studying, training and working in the world of clinical psychology and with that came the opportunity to get really immersed in the clinic of Lacan and his version of psychoanalysis. When you spend a great deal of time looking through those particular lenses, it's hard to just stop cold turkey. It makes for an addictive kaleidoscopic experience.

I discovered this as I found myself gravitating back to the theatre at the dawn of the new century. I fell into a teaching gig. Six weeks each summer with an eager group of young gifted performers. I got to preach my gospel of collective creation—always a cause with me—but I also found Lacan creeping in, not so much in what I did—which largely involved introducing the students to the Vocal Sequence, a performance discipline codified by Herbert Blau and his experimental group KRAKEN[1]—but chiefly through an impulse both to write journals and to generate a collection of supplemental "educational materials." I was undergoing my own analysis at the same time which, no doubt, exerted its own influence.

As I continued to push my way into the decade carrying theatre and Lacan on my back, I started to take assorted excursions and side trips. The common factor for filing away all these forays into the bush was a name: *lacuna*. I started to assert there was this performing entity that called itself *lacunagroup*. I derived great enjoyment from the name. A lacuna is a hole in a manuscript, with the implication that at one time a bit of meaning was present that is now no longer available, and, further, if one is optimistic and committed to puzzling and pondering and even cyphering, the absence can be resolved, the meaning restored. It also makes me think of a tropical paradise, a place with a lagoon and a bar where, after a swim, you can get a drink served in a pineapple with a little umbrella. But, too, there is a slight dark threat that the hole cannot be filled or figured out. But a farther and more remote possibility, at the most giddy extreme, the actual definition of the thing for me is effaced and the hole is no longer a former presence but a forever constitutive gap, an inevitable and catastrophic jumping off the

---

1   References to the Vocal Sequence will pop up frequently in this volume. The definitive description of the Vocal Sequence can be found in Herbert Blau's essay "The Grail of the Voice," contained in *The Dubious Spectacle: extremities of theater, 1976-2000*, Minneapolis: Univ Of Minnesota Press, 2002.

rails. And, finally, as friends forever like to point out, in *lacuna* you can find *Lacan*.

lacunagroup was truly a coalition of the willing. Work was done. We even had a website. On it, I would continue to write: notes of encouragement, statements of principle, promptings to create, and improvisational experiments that sometimes involved only myself in a full-bore mode of mono-mythic-mania and sometimes included an entire chatroom of cohorts. It was all quite mad, really. Often it seemed that the only theatre taking shape, and I can't help but think of Herbert Blau here, was in the writing itself, in that act, as I sat in the dark of a totally indescribable but wholly inscribable space, enthralled by the incitements and traumatic accidents of thought thinking its own truth into existence. Then I remember: work, in fact, was done. People met and tried to create. We gathered on a platform we had constructed on top of a little rise and around which I had dug a narrow moat rippling with words. Sometimes on hot days we choked a bit on a stagnating stench, but otherwise it was okay.

I did believe there was a new way to find a theatre in the words. This belief had taken over since trafficking with Lacan. In the theatre of Lacan's version of psychoanalysis, there is nothing but language and speaking (and occasionally a couch). It is the classic arena of the Freudian "talking cure" but somehow more austere, more (and for this I might get letters) *ascetic*. You try to keep the distractions of theory out of the way. A wager is made which assumes the gravity of an ethical commitment, one which is vulnerable, certainly, to the condescending estimations of other therapeutic schools and to the affable dismissals from a certain kind of scientific outlook, but for analysts working this way the gamble is real and not taken lightly: to truly understand what is going on with patients, you make a commitment to follow the language: it has been around them and within them since their infancy; it helped build them; it's there and not going anywhere. The words know the neighborhood, the words helped build the neighborhood, the words carry around a great deal of history and information, they've seen it all. Some things the words will share readily, other things require a certain kind of effort and a certain finesse, a bit of *savoir faire*. Often the words know more than they care to reveal. Often they don't know they know. Or they only dream what they know. However, if you stay with the words, you are going find out a great deal. You might think of the word as a unique and particular type of neurotransmitter. Furthermore, with assistance of the words, repairs can be made. So whether you are the one on the couch or the one po-

iii

sitioned behind it at a proper distance, you are working with words. And playing. And cursing. And abusing. And loving. All with words. Taking them apart, turning them over, suspending them, watching them refract the light. It becomes a habit. No, to be honest, it becomes something of a compulsion. I brought that preoccupation with me back to the theatre, and I was going to find a way to make it do something interesting, to make it perform.

This desire to crack open words and perform within the innards was not limited to the theatre, however. I confess I got a bit nutty with social media. I adopted an interventionist approach in the way I would deploy posts, as if I was going to rely on the butterfly effect to turn one syntactical disruption into a collective crying out for utopia which would span the continents. I would pun. I would whip up Joycean Wakean frittatas of meaning. For most of one year I wrote a haiku a day. A well-observed vignette would also appear on occasion, crispy with ironies both daunting and daring. And so on. The impulse to churn out sentences moved faster than any reflex for cautious reflection. I think this quirk of mine was underlined and lampooned a bit when I was appointed to the office of Aphorist in the Lichtenbergian Society, another group alignment from that era whose members only took seriously the coupling of vaunting creative ambition with measured and consistent procrastination. In other words, it was a drinking society devoted to putting off projects and discussing the avoidance of art and the art of avoidance, all as a tribute to the malaise of selective inactivity that afflicted the career of Enlightenment polymath Georg Christoph Lichtenberg. I took it upon myself to take the joke of my appointment seriously (Lichtenberg's *Waste Books* do exist, after all) and doubled my production of epithets, aphorisms and hoaxes. *This is "How to do Things with Words"* could have been emblazoned on my banner or crest or stationary. I was insufferable.

As for the symptom I suffered while fidgeting in the gaps between the words—the theatre of *lacanagroup*—it ran its course with the decade. I now believe I can pinpoint its true end. While on a morning walk in May of 2010 I came across a storm drain.

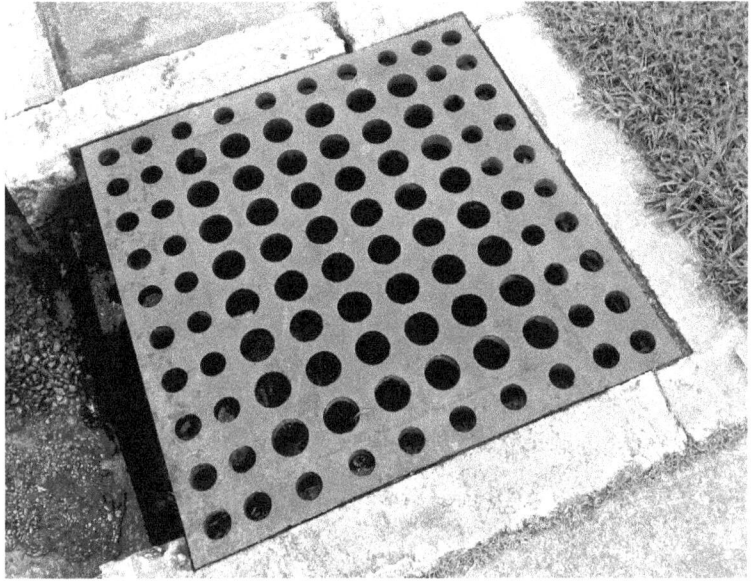

The first thing to note is that holes figure prominently in the clinic of Lacan. The presence of a "lacuna" in our name is certainly a nod to that. The drain set off a Lacan fantasia, really: to think of something being "full of holes" is a compelling paradox inasmuch as the in the clinic of Lacan the analyst is already encouraged to think in terms of lack or of empty sets or, alternatively, of fantasies of continuity and fullness. One hole. An infinity of holes. The vicissitudes of desire—to be without holes is to be without desire and to suffer the holes is the whole of desire. And then there's the psychotic horror of the holes as real, as so many unstoppable leaks, and of the terrifying loss of a distinction between outlets and inlets. But I also thought of O's. Letters. Also an important set of concerns with Lacan: the set of what can be written. Words, again, but now as galaxies of more elemental entities. Letters as the ins and outs of words. At a recent *lacunagroup* gathering there had been some discussion of resuming exploratory work on *King Lear*, so I found myself thinking of Shakespearean O's and the idea that the letter O held open a place in the script for some sort of extra-textual bodily outburst, for something unscriptable the actor had to evoke to further the unfolding meanings of character and action. I thought of a gully-washing flood of emotion which then led me to the quintessential instance of such an extra-textual actorly event in Lear's speech during the storm on the heath (BLOOOOOOOOW...). Storms, floods, tears, emptying out through the storm drain, through the O's. Eliotic O's of the "Shakespearean Rag" are in there too, of course, contending with endings. I also found myself reflecting on the elusive

V

twilight world of women and their O's, a subject so veiled and esoteric a poor Pentheus could only surreptitiously spy upon it through slapping and obscuring branches while contending with the ever-present risk of losing his head. The fantasia had shifted. Sexual difference, also an important category in the clinic of Lacan. EncOre. MOre. MOan. (MOM? the analyst silently and predictably ponders...) I was O-bsessing. NO surprise. I wondered if I could collapse this all into a name. A signifier. A MOttO? A mOniker? MOnica? That's all it took to conjure up the image of Harriet Andersson in Bergman's *Sommaren med MOnika*. It was quite a storm that was brewing and I wasn't sure if a sea of O's could drain it. The resulting text wrote itself. I brought it with me to our next *lacunagroup* (grOup grOpe grOOt grOttO...) meeting. (LakOOOOOOna LaOcOOn ...)

For *lacunagroup*

The TITLE: Storm Drain

The PERFORMERS: One or several.

The ACTIONS:

Face front. Connect.

vi

Turn around. Face away.

Turn around. Face front. Connect.

Turn to the right. Profile.

Turn back to the front. Connect.

Turn to the left. Profile.

Return to front. Connect. Complete.

(The ACTIONS may be performed as a sequence, or the items may be used singly or in groups, numerically ordered or not, interspersed between bits of TEXT or accompanying bits of TEXT.)

The TEXT:

Repeat after me.

O

OO

OOO

OOOO

OOOOO Monica

O Monica

O Monica, O Monica

OO Monica, O Monica

O Monica, OO

OO Monica, O Monica, O

O Monica Monica, O

Monica Monica, O Monica, O Monica

O Monica, O Monica, OO Monica

O Monica Monica Monica, O Monica, O

OO Mon-O-ica

Moni-O-ca

Mon-O-i-O-ca, O Mon-O-i-O-ca

Mon-O-i-O-O-ca-O, OO

O Mon-O-ica, O Moni-O-ca

O Mon-O-O-i-O-O-ca-O-O, O Monica, O

O Monica, your heart belongs to me.

To me your heart belongs, O Monica.

Your heart belongs, O Monica, to me.

O, to me your heart belongs, Monica.

O me, to your heart Monica belongs.

O me, Monica, to your heart belongs.

O me, your heart belongs to Monica.

O Monica, heart belongs me.

Monica, heart to.

O your heart.

O your belongs me.

O Monica, O your heart, O me.

Monica O me, heart your O, to O.

Monica, your belongs

Your belongs to me.

Belongs O belongs, your O me, heart O to.

O your O, belongs me O.

O Monica, your belongs, your belongs, to me, O me.

Me to belongs heart your Monica, O.

Monica to heart, O your me belongs.

Me belongs, Monica, O your heart to.

Me to Monica, heart belongs, heart belongs.

Monica me your, O Monica me your, heart O me your.

O Monica your O, O me to your heart.

Your to me O, Monica your heart.

Belongs to your Monica, me belongs.

Heart me to.

Heart me Monica.

Belongs me Monica.

O belongs, O me, O your O.

Your me, Monica.

Monica belongs to me, O your heart.

Me your, me your, me your, me.

Heart O, me your O, belongs, belongs.

O Monica, O heart me your belongs to.

Me your belongs, me your belongs, O.

Monica to me, O belongs, O belongs.

viii Monica, O.

Monica me

Heart belongs, to your, me to your.

Your to your, O me, Monica.

Your heart to your, O me, Monica

Heart Monica me, belongs your O, belongs your O.

Heart Monica your, me O belongs.

Moni-O-O-O-O

Ica-O-O-O-O

Ac-O-i-O-nom.

O Acinom O

A-ci-O-nom.

O O Acinom, O

O A O ci O nom O A

Om nom Om A i

O A i No m A i

O No A No ci No No No O

Ma No I C

M

A I C

O

A

N

OOOO

(The TEXT may be performed as a single sequence by a single performer with the ACTIONS employed when appropriate, or multiple performers may engage in contrapuntal processes with the TEXT and the ACTIONS. Repetitions and out-of-sequence combinations are possible. Remember to give time after each TEXT item for audience repetition—possibly excepting item 1 (*Repeat after me*). The audience interaction is a crucial part, performer interaction is optional. Other permutations which might supplement or extend the sequence of the TEXT are certainly possible.)

Neither I nor anyone else knew what to do with it. Even though I now have a lingering unashamed fondness for it, at that meeting I interpreted everyone's confusion as confirming that my marshaling of various Lacanian stratagems and preoccupations had hit a dead end. A periOd(d). An end to an era of effOrt. Furthermore, I suspected something else might be taking shape because I had brought a guitar and a broadly spacious metal bowl to the meeting and found my way towards playing them—tapping the now water-filled bowl while using it as a slide on the plucked guitar strings—in an attempt at accompaniment while I led us all singing some fragmented blues rendition of "The Old Oaken Bucket." (Old Oaken...still with the O's, thOugh nO mOre MOnica...) Sounds, voices, music, song: evidence I might be moving on to something else. There were a few more meetings, but I think that was it for *lacunagroup*. Maybe the absolute absence of the O was too much, maybe I wanted to plug the lacuna with something or at least find something to put there to smooth out the page. A little song and dance? It was a decade dOne. An era Over.

A few years later, Jeff Bishop, an always embarrassingly supportive *lacunagroup* cohort, presented me with a manuscript. He had spent some time online pulling together bits of my writings that were squirreled away in the archives of assorted blogs and other internet venues. He's an historian, after all. Raiding archives is what he does. He instructed me to publish. I consented with the added stipulation that I be allowed to include an Introduction...

(...*include an Introduction.* Here I want to pause. I was reviewing this Introduction, and as I passed through this moment of what can only be acknowledged as looping self-reflection, a folding back through repetition and re-examination, I decided there was an opportunity to make a cut and open a gap. I want to make an *interpretation*, a particular interpretation, and I feel a pressure to be the one who makes it. Pride, perhaps, is at work, and a bit of anticipatory defensiveness. I want to be the one to recognize what may the most obvious meaning beneath the presence of a lacuna. What's missing in this push towards a theatre? What may be absent is true creativity, and I can't allow myself to seem blind to that possibility. Many of the articles in this collection describe processes and approaches, a number of theoretical provocations, and numerous strategies and exercises, but little to no evidence of the thing itself. Sure, the ephemeral nature of performance can make isolating documentary evidence a difficult proposition, but in the case of this lacuna, the lack might be profoundly inevitable. My cohorts and I nervously pace around the opening, perhaps in denial. We wait for a birth, at least we hope for a crowning, for the first crowning of many crowns, for the children to appear and begin the journey, but the hole remains a hole. We circulate and wait. I theorize.

X

I may be struggling with that perpetual lack of a spark. Yes, in this collection you will find some evidence of creative effort, but I cannot help seeing each instance as a demonstration of merely the possibility of creativity. Not the actual thing but merely a *semblant*. No conception but deception. All with the best of intentions, but still. This is one interpretation of the lacuna. Now to resume my review of this Introduction. *I believe...*)

I believe he meant what he had assembled to come across as a self-portrait. It got me thinking and ultimately wondering whether or not that was truly the case. Dale Lyles, another *lacunagroup* member, created a cover. When I asked him about his choices, he confirmed what I had suspected: it was designed to make you think of a Grove Press paperback, as if what the reader was holding was one of those time bombs tossed from the barricades by the European theatrical avant-garde throughout the 1950s and 1960s, one of those collections of plays and essays that had certainly exploded my teenaged brains and left me with no hope for life save through a rebirth in the theatre. I appreciated the joke, and so, yes, the idea of a portrait of a sort, the idea that I, too, was another heroic exploder in the theatre, but this time without the reward of a real mOment, without a result as true as some Great GlObe itself Offering fOrth an era or even as palpably fully empty as a great Beckettian NOt-quite-NOdding-Off before the end. The era here was errOr maybe. Or it came before it went. Nothing could be found. NOthing.

So, in reality, maybe not a portrait after all. Too much absent. Too many holes. Something else may be going on. I want to end here by asserting that what was really scribbling through the decade in and on a theatre of absence was the *sinthome*. Those reading this who are familiar with Lacan may acknowledge that I've gone too far at this point. I ask them to bear with me. My appraisal of these "occasional writings" simply couldn't stay away from this idea. The *sinthome*², the word an archaic version of *symptom*, is a theoretical formulation which enabled Lacan toward the end of his teaching life to describe a certain kind of *self* (not a word he would use, *self*, really, but it makes for a quick explanation) engaged in an ongoing project of self-creation or self-writing, as if the act of creation could tie together and strengthen other registers of life and reality that are not coordinating for that self as they might. So not a summation, not a portrait. This was an engagement, a cycle set on perpetual spin, a span of years and Occasions: 2000-2010, a tying together, a binding up and rebuilding around some questions of self. I genuinely do still take my interest in Lacan seriously, and I present here what ultimately strikes me as some work on the *sinthome* that I have tried to accomplish through the *sinthome*. I hope it can be appreciated as a unique and colorful exploration of the concept. I also hope it has produced some diverting documentation.

Marc Honea

Newnan, Georgia

May 2014

---

2 The *Sinthome*? Really? To claim to discern the workings of the sinthome in one's own efforts is either delusional, hubristic, harebrained, or something worse not even worthy of an adjective. I am, however, compelled to make the claim, and I invite readers familiar with Lacanian concepts—along with readers of goodwill who are generally curious—to pursue the implications. Themes of identity and absence, of creativity pursued as self-creation, questions relating to the insubstantiality of the body and the Other's inscription (paternal and otherwise), a certain cycling repetition of action and "enjoy-meant" at work in working with words, the seeming necessity of investing in a name, and a priority for the name to be a naming of the (w)hole—for me the threads are there, but this a collection of writings, not a treatise, so I'm not pursuing it further in the pages to come. I encourage readers who want a more thorough introduction to the concept to try: Thurston, Luke, ed., *Re-inventing the Symptom: Essays on the Final Lacan*, New York: Other Press, 2002. And, if you are truly interested in learning more, in the Fall of 2016 (I am updating this note as we approach a publication date—it's currently the Spring of 2016), a published English version of Lacan's Seminar XXIII, *The Sinthome*, translated by Adrian Price and edited by Jacques-Alain Miller, will be available from Polity.

Don't we want once and for all to forget who we thought we were for all those years? But if we finally do forget, don't we still wish we had forgotten at least twenty years earlier?

1

"Why work in the Theatre? Because it's the one opportunity afforded us to make life somewhat interesting."

Another Farewell to the Theatre

I am in the process of carrying through on some emotional house-cleaning, and, as a part of that, I want to include a farewell to theatre-making. Not a grand, sweeping goodbye, I assure you, just a nod of farewell to a very particular set of concerns, to my own little peculiar domain of interest. I'm saying goodbye to the few notions of theatre-making I've attempted to explore, unsuccessfully, for the last twenty-three or so years. I want to briefly describe them, for the record, and then acknowledge my inability to realize them. Perhaps they are not really worth realizing, but I'll stop short of asserting that. I'm still too fond of the notions to go that far.

I want to keep it simple. These notions are simple. They are the shortest avenues I can imagine to pure stimulation. In the end, that may be the problem. I wasn't necessarily interested in the complexities and deferrals of story. But can theatre-making dispense with story? I wanted to fashion stimulating events composed of human presence, focused microscopically through the material reality of bodies, voices, and feeling. I make it sound O so heroic, don't I? But viable? Playable?

When you see a production of a play or musical or opera and you respond to a performance and a specific performer, you are at a precise distance to receive what you could call a certain *gestalt*, a masterful coordination of elements within a storied framework which illuminates a featured instance of human agency. You can call it "the power of a performance." You, the audience, the appreciative receiver, need the distance for the *gestalt* to cohere and work the way it does. The theatre-making that intrigued me involved reducing the distance to the performance just enough for the *gestalt* to fragment and collapse. The performer is now a heterogeneous swirl of elements, elements which can picked through and re-aligned or juxtaposed or collided into a new kind of event.

Voice, for instance. I really like listening to voices doing strong and unusual things. I like the experience of a voice dispensing with amplification and projecting into a space. I like the strange turns and distortions in such a voice. I like to experience remarkable textures in a voice. It's a vocal encounter that only works in the here and now, however. If it's recorded, preserved, or mediated in some way, it might as well be a curio preserved in a jar of formaldehyde. It's dismissed as an instance of outdated oddness that can only collect dust on the shelf. But it's evident that striving to produce such elements in a voice leads the speaker into unusual and challenging emotional terrain. The audience is taken to new territory in the listening. I wanted to make theatre in which such an element is not a background "gift" or quality of a performer (or an instance of embarrassing excess), but is part of the focused stimulating event. The performer brings it to bear through a kind of imposed immediacy.

Voice is just one element, one example. Embodiment. Movement. Manner of relational approach. Modes of intimacy. These all float and hover and offer themselves for new configurations. The performer willfully moves through the options in this strange disarticulated collection of possibilities. This is the stuff of the theatre-making I attempted.

4 Why could I never make it go anywhere in a fully satisfying way? I could offer any number of reasons, but I recently hit upon the chief reason, something that colored everything else, that explains much of what I see as a failure of will.

I thought I knew what I wanted to do, *but I was afraid of what I thought I wanted to do.*

I feared the very radical strangeness of what I wanted to pursue.

As you can imagine, it made surmounting the resistance of others rather difficult.

But there we have it. My statement of intent. My nod of goodbye. I leave it for other more muscular imaginations. Or if it is just a cluster of impossibilities knotted out of my past and could never be a viable route for theatrical exploration and expression, I can now simply set it aside.

I'm done fiddling with it.

Pretend it's really all a Grand & Glorious Adventure.

These days every walk is a walk
through the historic district on a cold day.
But memory is that best, most favorite coat.
Fists warming in my pockets,
eyes wet, half shut on familiar sites.
The unpredictable pummeling of air
is now exhilarating,
and I press into it.

It's 14" by 62" by 1.25" and weighs...a lot. I came across it while on a walk. It was lying on a curb. I'm thinking it had been tossed as trash. I had my phone with me, so I took a picture. It stayed there on the curb another two weeks. I kept telling myself I should drive by and pick it up. Finally, after two weeks, I did. That's when I discovered it was heavy.

I'm inclined to think the board was part of a saw table. The straight and circular bites into the plywood are deep.

How does this object affect me? When I try to answer that question, the first association I make is to the work of Anselm Kiefer. The length of it, the stretch, evokes the horizon, or a monumental vista, or some span across a mind numbingly long cosmic stretch of time. I think, too, of the merging of myth and material in Kiefer. It's a material torn from the earth. It's imposed upon rather than fabricated or tooled. It's forced to be a witness to the oldest of stories.

In my various interests, the ones in particular that force my Lacanian hand, the word "inscription" appears a good deal. Coupled often with "cut." It's the cut that makes meaning. The cut or incision on something too real, in an effort to get it to be read or apprehended as experience. These rings and lines and wrinkles evoke a fundamental motion that is the dance of particles, of energy, the trails followed in the depth of all matter and all life. By what? Who knows? We inscribe as a way to see it. It inscribes us. We inscribe it. It's wood. It's skin. It's the dance at the place where wood and skin are the same.

Cave writing. Aboriginal art. Particle trails in cloud chambers. The segue-ways during *The Big Bang Theory*. Eroded channels of water. Trade lanes on impossible hermetic maps. The scars and fractal flashing of Lichtenberg lightning. All there.

I'm more a Responder than a Creator, I think. All I can do is look at this thing and wish I had made it.

The lecturer, motivated by a strange mixture of fascination and disgust and by an interest in connecting with this student, interrogates her on the nature of gum chewing, its physical mechanics, its pleasures, the decision to remove and dispose of it, etc. In phenomenological detail. The audience watches this exchange either chewing their own gum or having chosen not to chew, some having thought they might "save it for later," some not chewers, etc. Lecturer starts out trying to humiliate the student and prove gum chewing is a sign of second-rate intellect, but the exchange goes in unexpected directions lecturer cannot control. Lecturer has already placed a call for something to be done about all the gum under the chairs, hence the arrival of "the scraper."

8

Stop. Deep breath. Unclench hand. Wiggle fingers. Resume.

Put Things into Play (and, after later theoretical reflection, *vice versa*)

Why do I dwell on "meanings," maps, charts, links, words, linguistic nuance, even when what we are about in performance is actions?

The Lacanian turn in psychoanalysis was to assert that this activity on the Other stage obeys not the laws of biology but language. It's a bold, non-intuitive claim, and one that is hard to "prove" without giving, also, a taste of the psychoanalytic experience as a referent. That's very difficult.

What I would say is this. What do symbol systems allow us to do? Very simply, they allow us to PUT THINGS INTO PLAY. And because of the nature of such systems, some of the play is autonomous. We have conscious influence, but the system also runs on its own, employing an integral system of movement, transformation, "energy" (Freud had no other way to think about it at the time). Let's use the old fashioned term libido just because it is very evocative and has a useful condensing aspect. Our libido relies on symbolic operations to…function. It is not purely "cellular" or "instinctive." In fact, to the extent that we can acknowledge the workings or vicissitudes of a libido, we are acknowledging something that is defined by the reality of symbolic activity, of things PUT INTO PLAY.

9

So when we explore and then review and re-express, we are using "meanings" to portray the very simple truth of our drives and desires AT PLAY. We are attempting to discern some of those hidden, autonomous, symbolic exchanges that allow us (as libido, if you will) to be.

Obviously, I am not talking about the propositions of medical science, but neither am I poo-pooing them. I am not talking about a more traditional "psychological" approach, but I don't dismiss that either. But I digress at this point.

With a second mirror
you can see the corpse.

it must be tough keeping house when neither knows how to do the irony.

interior fears and inferior tears.

it's always strange when everything is in and out of reach equally.

11

Starting a
Performance Group

This material is aimed, in part, at those of you interested in starting performance groups and creating original work. Some of the material borrows from my own days of training in methods influenced by Herbert Blau's experimental group KRAKEN and some from my own attempts to adapt those methods to the teaching of high school theatre students at the Georgia Governor's Honors Program.

Collective creation in the theatre is simply my cause, collective creation of all kinds. I believe the work of groups creating original performance pieces needs to continue as a vital aspect of theatrical expression, and while there is certainly no evidence that group expression is dying in the theatre worldwide (a former student just sent me a report on a recent Edinburgh Festival he attended and… "wow," he said), I worry that young theatre artists in our culture are not being led down certain possibly fruitful paths or are being offered very trivial experiences in group development. I worry that vital group expression in the theatre, in this country, is on its way to becoming a chapter or two in Theatre History, a few quixotic moments of emergence now over and done with.

12

I am not trying to offer a set of pre-fabricated definitions and blueprints. Many of my contributions are simply addressed to the question: If you can get a number of performers to agree to be in a room together, how might you get things started? Because of the influence of KRAKEN on my work, much of what I'm offering is designed to invite performers to look within, both as performers and by performing, and to offer the search, the discoveries, and the attending thoughts as possible moments of ensemble expression. You need not, however, go the way of KRAKEN-like navel gazing to create group work or use the materials I offer.

One invitation I want to make explicit: A group of high-school age actors can use group creation as an interesting alternative for one-act competition. All you need are a group of interested students, a teacher's permission, scheduled time, and a place to work. My hope is that such adventurous groups can use this website as a means of sharing information and experiences.

My one worry as I've been assembling these materials, and it's a worry I never managed to escape working as a teacher, is that my offerings are all too indirect to be useful. I do not present a how-to manual. Many students have never witnessed a really compelling or powerful original piece of performance created by an ensemble and so have no frame of reference. They just don't know what such a thing might look like. Perhaps they need a script of some kind or a set of step-by-step instructions to get started or some kind of guidance on texts and materials.

The only way I have found to respond to these worries (since I have no plans of putting together a how-to manual) is to view the "leap into the unknown" as the best source of energy for the group and the strongest glue for holding it together. Suddenly matters of taste and material merge with the existential and the ethical. Thoughts of hanging together or hanging separately and the focus of minds knowing they may hang tomorrow all become incredibly influential. Honesty and urgency and true originality take on fresh value.

13

Comments during an online rehearsal

One thing nice about the way we're going about this is that we can continually review what has been said or done and begin to make charts or maps that will then provide a blueprint for making a piece.

Psychoanalysis wagers that in addition to our "performing," interacting, creating, questioning, there is another scene, another stage. Each of us acts with our own other scene in play. It is a scene beyond our conscious control and one that behaves in ways out of reach of our desire to deploy or regulate. Where it is, we are not.

The scene is individual and subjective at first. As we explore, we offer bits and pieces of meaning which perhaps touch upon this Other scene (all bits of meaning do, even if only remotely or through covering or complication). Our gaffs and goofs and stalling can, of course, touch upon that scene more directly. Those, too, are part of the mix.

14 Each of us offers our own meanings while responding to the meanings of others as we play and explore. The idea of a *symptomatic atmosphere* is that we begin to share constellations of meaning around the bits we share. We begin, perhaps, to implicate one another in our other scenes. What might this mean?

To an extent, all we have to go on are these bits we generate. But we can only begin to speculate about the unconscious stuff by reviewing and then pushing forward with possible manipulations based on our reviews. Ultimately, I believe we are trying to create a performance event that somehow draws the audience into our same shared shadowy atmosphere. And we can be led to making some really interesting choices and decisions based on our dwelling with these shared meanings.

Let me try to give an example of how to play with meanings and find new connections.

Dale attempts to demonstrate his frightening, authoritarian voice and speaks to Jeff as if Jeff is a student. As an authority, Dale offers that he can see what is hidden, or at least sense the presence of what might be hidden. The gum under the chair. This notion of being able to see what's hidden gets worked through in another way later when Dale, in response to my deployment of "risk revealing," explores the vicissitudes of becoming naked in front of the audience. Did my use of "reveal" pick up on the notion of "seeing what is hidden?" My motive was to nudge Jeff toward unpacking more in connection with his "dare to be boring" comment. It inadvertently activated Dale's interest in what it means to reveal and conceal and to know it has taken place. Perhaps. This is just a proposal of linkages. I have left out a great deal of complexity just to give a quick illustration.

Everything we add to the mix unfolds numerous possibilities. The sardines memory was triggered by the appearance of gum under the chair and the "gross" idea of eating it in a sandwich. But I also use that story because I believe it says something about my nature, about a certain kind of passivity. I earlier alluded to a "paralysis." It also touches upon the notion of people sharing something "disgusting." And how I fancy myself as someone more inclined to both offer and receive something disgusting. The ambiguity of Jeff's scraping comes into play here. Is he harvesting? Cleansing? Aggressively cutting into the proceedings? Is he exploring the notion that he can somehow remove the hidden secret that Dale, as Master, could perceive?

Our choices also touch upon the drives, those things "beyond the body" in a psychoanalytic sense. Think of the ways we have engaged the eyes, the mouth, the ear. Jeff's choice to act silently with his toolbox is interesting. It can be interpreted as a strong instance of anal aggression. The drives are in play; they too are a part of our shadowy scenes.

A long digression. But I was very excited while cutting the grass the other day and I went into a revery concerning how even with the small network of ideas we've begun to explore, we could make some fun playing choices. A play? A performance event? Something very concrete in terms of presence and action, but also something that triggers an unsettling mystery.

Whenever I hear the word Culture, that's when I reach for my checkbook.

Great-Aunt Lucretia on a certain bridge partner: "My God, the woman ain't just loud, she's Alabama loud."

A Dear in the headlights of Demand.

Doom and gloom. Who and whom.

"The clown whittles it down bit by bit just to spite those who stand ready with their tape measures."

"Show an interest in others? My dear, if life were twice as long, that might begin to be a possibility."

The mere desire to aspire
and already I long to retire.

What is the Event?

The proverbial empty space. The eternally expectant audience. An interval. An actor enters carrying a chair and sets it before the audience. Leaves. An interval with added nuance. Our already thoroughly expectant audience is now perhaps even moreso. An actor enters and sits in the chair. Now an interval with fresh enhancements.

What is the event?

In school I was apprenticed to an artist who asked that question constantly. He purposely invested it with a Zen-like mystery. We were the suitably thick-headed grasshoppers: Well, tell us what an "event" is and we, eager to please students that we are, will answer your question.

No response. An *event* was an *event* when it was *self-evident*. Many an actor would then try to talk his or her way into something. And retreat from any grasp of the event. Directors and playwrights were not safe. They, too, were asked the question. The event was the essence of the matter. And the essence was mysterious and hard to articulate, but our teacher conveyed the conviction that this essence was the core of our work in the theatre. The audience and the event. The heart of the matter.

"What is the event?" Ask the actor sitting in the chair.
"I am waiting for her to arrive. I need to tell her something. The truth. I intend to tell her the truth. Why isn't she here? I sit and wait." After the actor gives the above response one can still follow up with "But what is the event?" What can the actor say now? And will it be a touch defensive? What is the event? Does the audience see the actor waiting? Or see the character waiting? Do we say that what the audience sees depends on the story or the given circumstances? Does it depend on the truth that the actor intends to tell? Do we need to know such things to talk about the event? The question triggers reflections and more questions.

Re-read the first paragraph.

The writing attempts to describe a situation and a series of…. events? It attempts to give an account from a particular point of view. Whose? Is the writer a member of the audience? Was the writer even present on the occasion? Is the whole thing made up? Just a series of illustrative descriptions in a highly self-conscious tone? Is the writer the actor? And could the actor be reflecting back on the occasion? Or is this a depiction of the actor's experience as it happened? Too objective to belong to the actor? Is the description scrupulous to detail, detached, sparse, what? And what is the event?

You may think it silly to say, "The event was my re-reading the first paragraph and then jumping down and reading the previous paragraph and now reading this one." But you are correct to note that an event is different from a description of an event. Not silly or precocious in the least to make that observation. You, in fact, were the agent in that event. The cause. The human cause. You were prompted to be the agent by some instructions you read, but that is just a complication, a little extra agency behind the scenes.

Re-read the previous two paragraphs.

Nestled in those paragraphs are little bits of reflection which, if gathered together in a certain way, contain a foolish attempt to define the theatre event. You take a moment to gather them up and see what coheres.

Here's my version of the attempt: an event in the theatre is any human activity which facilitates experiences of memory, thought, communication, or emotion. It seems self-evident enough, but its origin is rooted in what struck me as singular: *an event is what inspires historians.* What does an historian work with? Such observations and questions can lead to thinking about the event as some moment of experience which is capable of writing its way into us and remaining. An event, then, is what people experience or witness in such a way that something about it gets inscribed in memory and so becomes available for future use. An event has something about it which is transferable, like a love note passed in the back of the classroom. An event is a moment with a shelf-life. An event travels time and space through the traces it leaves in our minds.

18

To ask "What is the event?" is a way to find what has remained after the moment is over. Has what just happened left anything for memory, thought, communication, or emotion? You might ask an actor, "Are you making an event?" Or "What are you going to do to make this an event?" "What are you going to do that memory can hang onto?" It may sometime be the case that asking "What would my character do in this situation?" is not going to yield enough fruitful material, particularly if the resulting actions do not have clarity as events. It is not necessarily stepping out of the moment or the relationship to think in terms of events. It's not necessarily "playing to the audience." It's not just the audience's memory you are concerned with. You can also attempt to give something to a stage relationship that will travel with it or even alter it.

Simple activities on a stage can be invested with an awareness of event as a way to dispel tentative or incoherent behavior and speech. Use a focus on the event as a way to get to the vital reality. The actor walks out and sits in the chair. Is it an event? Is the action writing itself into history? Is something getting inscribed which sits in the gut? Did something get written into the actor's memory at that moment?

To speak of the event also allows for a way to approach more abstract or experimental types of performance. We can imagine creating performances through a building up of events, a sequencing of events, a coordination of events. Events may serve a narrative. Events may harmonize in a particular way to serve a narrative, but it might be possible to re-arrange events, to re-harmonize within a narrative, or to arrange events which reach to the audience audience both within and outside an evolving narrative structure. Since a narrative helps inscribe events into a workable history, to serve up events outside a traditional narrative is to open new areas to the processes of memory, thought, communication, and emotion, calling on new non-narrative possibilities for organization. Or if you believe we are all narrative all the time, events in radical composition may reveal new narratives.

SUGGESTIONS

19

- Rehearse any material with an event awareness. See what happens.

- Take an anecdote or tale or fable. Create a series of events which serve the narrative drive of the story in the clearest possible way.

- Compose an arrangement of events and allow the story to weave its way through as a presence, but focus most of the events on evoking unspoken or emotional or atmospheric undercurrents discovered in your unfolding responses to the story.

- Create an event poem without narrative support.

Let me quickly take stock

The most significant thing I can say at this point is I've let myself go astray from my original drive to undertake this work through my preferred theoretical avenues. It's funny. It's certainly ironic. I've become the word guy because my most pressing desire is to explore what in the theatre might be seen as unscriptable. My trauma, my delirium, my ghost, my fatality, they all involve my experiences working in a fashion in which what is unspeakable in the spoken is what takes the focus, in which enigmatic events unfold and ask to be newly assimilated. It's pretty much my wordless mystical core. It's a set of sentinel events.

I'm attempting to formulate strategies for negotiating through such unspeakable intensities, and I have eschewed conventional psycho-physical performance languages revolving around "the body" in an effort to find new things.

Hard to do in a blog. Not impossible, though. My approach involved focusing on the activity we were engaged in: we were all imagining events and choosing words to describe those events. What might be enigmatic and unscriptable in that? In our attempts to write? In an effort to get at it, I couldn't stay within the scenario we were describing. In the absence of intensities playing out in a physical space, I explored possible intensities lurking in our writing. And I used the same "psychoanalytic methods" I was interested in employing in work in an actual space.

Problem is, I couldn't successfully transmit my ways of strategizing and "interpreting." I began to stand in a corner and try to talk my way out. Still not practical enough. I need to offer more than a mindset.

There. I think others may see my stretches of being "rational" as endpoints and, therefore, not in service of fruitful creativity. But they're certainly not meant to be endpoints. Back to my memories of the unspeakable. I must hold that in view. The mystical vision.

Make a Talisman

During some of my down time one summer as a drama teacher at GHP, I began to work with something I'm going to call a *Talisman*, constructed using an ordinary Scrabble board and set of tiles. The adventure of constructing a Talisman is in sympathy, I'm going to claim, with some of the experiences of being in psychoanalysis. It's in no way the equivalent of a psychoanalytic journey, but I'm claiming it is an entertaining way to undergo an encounter with one's desire through the agency of letters, words, and signifiers. It's a subjective experience with some of Lacan's concepts, a quasi-psychoanalytic encounter with the "desire of the Other." Consider it an opportunity to have a private adventure of "self-discovery" tinged with a psychoanalytic flavor.

You need not construct your Talisman all in one sitting. My first attempt took shape over a number of days. To begin the process, set out the Scrabble board and place all of the tiles face down and close by.

Turn over one tile.

It's a letter (if it's blank, discard and turn over another, I've chosen not to use the blanks for this exercise). It has made its appearance randomly. You place it on the board anywhere you choose. At this point in the adventure, it's simply there to remind you that the *letters* were already there before *you* were. You existed as a signifier, a unit of meaning, a "letter," for others before you began to acquire meanings for yourself. Letters, the stuff of meaning, come first, and many contingent encounters with them will take place before your "choice" enters into the picture. The unconscious is already at play. Eventually you will make some word around the letter you've place on the board and assure that the word links with all of the other words, but you don't have to do that right away.

Turn over three tiles. The method for constructing the Talisman is as follows. You want to fill up the Scrabble board with as many interlinking words as possible. When you are done, each word in the Talisman has to be attached to another as in a crossword puzzle, but unlike the game Scrabble proper, you do not have to link words as you go. You can place an un-linked word on the board as long as you find a way to link it before you end your work on the completed Talisman. If you cannot link the word eventually, you must remove it. The first letter you turned over must wind up in a word constructed around it at its location on the board, and that word must link to another by the time you complete your work. You can build a word around the letter and link at any time.

The crossword-like linking of letters and words is meant to evoke the chains of signifiers which exist in the unconscious. The demands of language forge certain links, others can come about through association, accident, assonance, homophony, metaphorical relations, and some come about through multiple combinations of all of those processes and others. Our subjective experiences of memory and thinking are two phenomena contoured in part by these chains of signification. These chained signifiers also hold a great deal of emotional and bodily experience.

At this point in your work on the Talisman, you can only have three tiles turned up at a time. To reveal other letters, you will have to return upturned tiles to their face-down positions. Only three letters can be revealed at any one time.

You want to fill the board with *powerful* words. "Powerful" in whatever sense has meaning for you. You can also spell out people's names. You can use any language (but try sticking to commonly recognized languages). No one else will see the words, so try and assemble words that evoke honestly powerful responses. The words can consist of any number of letters. You can only see three letters upturned at any given time, however, as you go about assembling. You must use memory as you search through tiles for the letters you want. Remember, too, that all the words you assemble have to link up by the completion of your work. One final, possibly controversial, guideline: the words do not necessarily have to be spelled correctly; if it evokes the word through pronouncing related sounds (*tayl* instead of *tail*, for instance, or *witnis* instead of *witness*), that's fine. I'll offer my explanation for this freedom a bit further on in these instructions.

As you proceed you will discover that, yes, the process becomes a combination of deliberation, accident, and expedience. Now then, give yourself some time to work this exercise before you read further in these instructions. Try to pay attention to your actual ordeal. Note where you decide upon words and begin to search for the completing letters. Note your compromises and disappointments. Note your triumphs. Note the associations the words themselves begin to trigger. Note where you do debate over use of proper spelling. Note how placing words in close proximity can also lead to associations, memories, stories, feelings, etc. Seriously, stop and take some time with the exercise; I don't want my promptings to work like "suggestions." It needs to be a personal and subjective experience.

Another guideline to take into account. When you feel that you have gone as far as you can go overturning only three letters at a time, you can begin to turn over five at a time. Note when and how you decide to move to this "lessened restriction." Note, too, that in order to proceed you may have to start studying that place on the board where the total number of tiles for each letter is listed. You have to avoid running out of what you need. Stay aware of your triumphs and compromises. Note how you are interpreting "powerful."

Before you call the Talisman completed, you may turn up seven letters at a time if you wish. How do you feel about the words assembled with the "three tile" method when you compare them with the "five tile" words and the "seven tile" words?

I want to liken the process of assembling the Talisman to the experience of encountering one's desire in the psychoanalytic sense. Lacan might say that desire exists in the Symbolic. In other words, desire is something shaped through law and restriction. We can only pursue that which can be "signified" in some way. And in the Symbolic we can only find those things which, ultimately, the letter is going to allow us to find. This is not just about our experiences of frustration, though part of desiring involves the experience of something 23 being not quite it. Often we can be surprised by what the signifiers are holding together for us, particularly as we move away from our controlled conscious awareness and into other chainings and links at work under the radar. Think about those moments of anticipation and frustration as you began furiously flipping through the tiles (if you had such moments). So much excitement over a few letters. Think about the little games you played with yourself as you decided upon which words to pursue.

Read through your completed Talisman. How do you as a reader begin to play with the words? Do any surprising juxtapositions lead to unexpected thoughts? Or do you find yourself nodding in verification over every connection? What's it like to think of other phrases or sentences implied by the contiguity of words? Do "rude" words ever collide with "idealistic" words or people's names?

Why don't I insist on proper spelling? To avoid having your first experience of making a Talisman compromised by my ruminations and opinions, hold off on reading the rest of this paragraph until your first Talisman is complete. Didn't I say desire involves our experiences with laws and restrictions and how we accommodate them? Why not insist on proper spelling to impose another set of limits and frustrations? Part of the psychoanalytic wager contains the belief that our earliest experiences with language are primarily shaped by what we hear, that we build up sonic associations before we begin to link them to letters. (For those earliest experiences we are at the mercy of what others do with letters.) It's interesting, I think, to have to negotiate the pursuit of a word with the pressure to respect spelling. Does the disregard of spelling constitute "giving in" to some other priority? Or is it an attempt to access a more primordial state of being, a more fundamental encounter with one's "mother tongue?" I want to liken it to an analysand's experience with the question of what can or can't be said to the analyst. Often, too, an analysand's work with a particular word or signifier may turn on a pun or a likeness shared among vowels, consonants, or within some other aural association. Certain common sounds might evoke a whole cluster of meanings. You might even try reading your Talisman with an "ear" toward hearing certain repeating sounds, vowels, consonants. Might such sounds have significance?

But I don't want to neglect the eye. Obviously some of your words will inspire images as will some of the juxtapositions of those words. Contained, too, in the psychoanalytic wager, is the belief that the learning of letters is linked with a child's attempts to understand some of the mysteries he or she has encountered in early childhood experiences. Yes, one might even go so far as to assert that a particular letter's shape can tell a child something about a parent's strange or inexplicable actions, etc. As an objective notion, it's pretty far-fetched, but as a possible subjective and imaginative experience, it certainly can happen. And not just in the mind of a child.

Keep your completed Talisman on hand for a few days. Return to it from time to time. Read it. Let it read you. At some point, if you wish to pursue further creative games which I will include here in the future, write the words down somewhere.

Resolves evolve, revolve, dissolve.

"Use of ampersand is charming. But ultimately easier? I'm skeptical. Fingers have to do more complicated things. Sort of same as my disenchantment with sober sex."

addicts protest in vein

the constant interplay: revealing and congealing.

a surfeit of stimulation can end with a word (or three)

25

Family Freud!

That's Intertwinement!

it's perfect weather to strike the hot ironist a while.

there's no risk of anything half-baked these days.

notes on method: put the pun in puncture; point at inflated egos.

notes how gatekeeping is now delicious while traveling is now suspicious.

A "parent survey" response for my daughter's English class on the topic of internet supervision

Whenever I come upon my sixteen year old daughter absorbed in her laptop, I am expected to play my part in a set routine. My daughter created it, and because she is a comedian, it's a pithy and concise bit of Vaudeville schtick. As a parent I can't help but be proud, even though she gives herself the funny stuff and expects me to embarrass myself as the hapless straight man.

Goes something like this. I wander by. She remains motionlessly consumed in whatever is on her laptop. I stop. I turn and look at her as though I'm trying to recollect something I know I need to tell her. There's a pause. Then maybe I mutter something like, "Oh, by the way…," as if I just remembered what it was I wanted to say. In one swift and deft move she looks up at me as she slams shut her laptop's screen. She gives me this…stare. It's questioning and subtly malevolent at the same time. It's the twist in the bit, the comic turn. Even though I am not even remotely interested in what's on her laptop, even though I might or might not idly try to glance at the screen as I pause with my question, she, with her move and her…stare, transforms me, whether I'm glancing over her shoulder or not, mind you, into a dirty creeper who is trying to peer into her world. She's the one who slams shut the laptop, but I am the pervert. Come on! Who's really guilty, and of what? There's no escaping that I'm clearly the dupe of this routine. I walk right into the trap. She's minding her own business and then I come along with my aging vampiric desire, attempting to feed on her innocent youthful enjoyment. How dare I? *Yes? What? May I help you?* I bluster and protest that I have no interest in what she's looking at. She continues the… stare. I stand guilty. I should be ashamed. It's a great bit.

Classic schtick. However, like any comic routine, if you turn it slightly and look at it out of sync with its working tempo, you realize it is a ritual. It's a ritual my daughter and I enact every time she sees me seeing her with her laptop, as if that moment demands we enact some significant understanding.

What do we understand in those moments? I think it's rather complex, and the ritual itself, couched in comedy to countenance a large component of anxiety, played out in full each time, is the only way to fully write what all is going on. One of the things rituals do--to play amateur anthropologist for a moment--is combine a number of contradictory impulses, equivocal ideas, and mixed motives into a concrete series of repeatable and reconcilable actions. Repetition refines a chaotic mess of both malignant and ecstatic emotions and allows for more ponderable meanings and manageable sensations to take shape. Think of the handshake. I touch the flesh of someone who is a stranger to me. That in itself is a bold gesture. One doesn't usually make to touch an other one does not know. Am I offering friendship or testing the strength of a potential threat? Am I filling a moment of awkwardness and uncertainty? Am I establishing a provisional truce or creating an alliance? Checking for weapons? Opening myself to another? The ritual handshake writes the complexity of all of these possibilities, and with a quarter-turn back, it, like every ritual, has the potential for comedy: just note how not being ready for a quick, strong handshake immediately can turn you into a pathetic, farcical, doubting mess.

I think that in the terse comedy of the laptop routine my and daughter and I carry through a ritual just as complex, and I think it revolves around something profound the computer has brought into the parent-child relationship. Why not put it starkly in the language of the Old Testament? Computers bring the Knowledge of Good and Evil. Not that this wasn't there before computers, of course. Nothing new under the sun, to use more Old Testament language, but maybe, thanks to computers, the not-new is now more immediate.

Handling these matters has always been a miserable parental burden, and part of most parents' strategy, I think, has always focused on timing. We try to temper the truth of the Fall by going slowly. We try to feed in the darker facts of life gradually. Our language evolves through the years of maturation. Maybe we bring the remote troubling mood of a fairy tale a touch closer as we issue our warnings about that street too far from home or that stranger who isn't going to tell you the truth. We dance about with the talk of "bad people" or of kids who might try to talk them into doing "things they really don't want to do." Time, access, and distance were more in our control as we led them by the hand to peek behind certain creaky doors or at figures recumbent under pale linen shrouds. We let the moment and necessity and growth guide us. Before computers.

Now the entire enormity of the human condition waits right on the other side of a squarish or oblong portal sitting on a desk in our home or resting in our child's lap. Lies offered as truths. Truths offered as lies. Facts offered as fun. Friendly persuasion. And evil incarnate. All of it there, now, no waiting. For us, the parents, time is no longer on our side. The monster has crawled out from under the bed.

Because of the computer, my daughter and I had talks before I was ready to have them, before she was ready to have them, too, probably. Long talks. Detailed. I had to work hard to summon effective and useful metaphors. I had to use starker images. More immediate. Less ambiguous. More proximate. Implicating all that was both familiar and foreign. I issued prohibitions that were non-negotiable. I relativized notions like privacy, freedom, choice, maturity. I apologized to her for the fact that those concepts, once she sat down in front of the portal, were meaningless. Gazing into the portal, we would not pretend she was cultivating those things. Truly, we sat together and talked and beheld the Fall.

The laptop ritual acknowledges that. In a way, it's as if the computer brought trauma, and our little ritual is a way of turning such an upheaval into a fact of life. The computer also brought complexity, and the routine allows us to bring together the complexity into something manageable. It reminds us of what we had to sacrifice as we figured out how to make a place for the computer in our home. It implicates us in the sad truths of life. It torments us a bit with a warning that the beast is *really out there*. And *in here*. And it helps us tolerate the discomfort of having to share such things with one another before either one of us was ready. And it assures my daughter that I will still pry and indulge my suspicions. It allows her to assert her autonomy in spite of my having rendered her cherished notions of freedom and independence contingent and conditional. It also allows her to be angry at me. And thank me. At least I tell myself she is thanking me. She may just be calling me a creep with no life.

28

Freudian washed up on Jungian shores

Here's what I knew earlier today. On a piece of paper my father kept folded up in his wallet was a cartoon depicting an unhappy man sitting in a box. Hermit? Homeless? Definitely dour and dyspeptic. Cloaked and eternal. A monk who's focused effort has led to total en-darken-ment. A *Bodhisattva* sitting on the bottom line. Underneath the sketch was inscribed "People are no damn good." I don't remember the first time my father showed it to me. I was very young. It always tickled me. My father, I seem to remember, was not forthcoming with details, saying simply that he kept it because he found the image amusing. Someone had given it to him. Memory is unreliable, of course, but I think I carried away a feeling that he found the inscribed sentiment brutally true. I remember him referring to the figure as "some Chinaman living in a box." (Not really a racist comment, I realize, as I now examine the sketch and note it is really easy to mistake the extreme frown lines on the face for a stereotypical "Fu Manchu mustache.") My father would have been characterized by most who met him as a genial and pleasant guy, but this cartoon somehow resonated for him. That, at least, was the conclusion formulated by my younger self. I saw it as his secret truth.

I decided to take a few minutes and go online to find out more about the cartoon, to investigate, finally, a profoundly significant paternal signifier. Was this, perhaps, the very "Name of the Father" itself? In my perpetually inflated view, I was convinced I was going to start some journey of psychoanalytic investigation, work my rusty Lacanian chops, and end up with a charming but nonetheless challenging bit of literary autobiography. This little cartoon, with its corrosive brief assessment, had always functioned for me as a tiny banner of identity. I jokingly refer to it as my "birthright." And most people would probably characterize me as a genial and pleasant guy.

I tempered my anticipation, however, with the thought that it all may be for nothing. Along with seeing a profound amusing clarity in the sketch, I was also tempted to convince myself it was just bathroom banality, of the kind I imagined exchanged by young chuckling GI's from my father's war years (WWII). Nothing more than that. An arbitrary item, collected for no other reason than the enjoyment of seeing "damn" in print.

So, warily, I began to investigate. First I discovered that the artist was William Steig. Yes, of *Shrek* fame (the creator of), but also famed as one of *The New Yorker*'s premiere cartoonists and illustrators through the second half of the twentieth century. I am exultant to think of my father carrying around a Steig cartoon. It flatters my ego. But I also realize he may not have known who Steig was. The cartoon first appeared on a best-selling "studio card" from around 1940. So it was ubiquitous. The *Shrek* of the moment. The refined had been tempered, or brought back to earth, by the everyday. Was bathroom banality winning out? I begin to work up to a theme. I noted, also, that my knowledge of Steig was, until I began exploring today, superficial. I did not know that I should have been "in the know" about Steig before I began looking into him. That, too, fit with the self-portrait I was seeking and would fit nicely with the themes that began to simmer. Banality, deficit, pretense. Then, in search of more appearances of the cartoon on the web, I googled a link...

http://post45.research.yale.edu/archives/904

30 This is where it gets bizarre. And to fully appreciate how bizarre, I have to make some confessions. I have a few quirky interests. We all do, I realize. Nothing seriously off the map, I can assure you. No doubt we all have a collection of topics or themes which inevitably trigger our curiosity should we see them referenced in a book title or in a magazine or online. Some of mine, many of mine, were all linked together in a network of associations in the article above, all reflecting my desire to peep into the lives of those who have made mad efforts to pierce the veil--creatively, sexually, politically, egoically. Wilhelm Reich, Kate Bush, Patti Smith and all of her *poète maudit* forbearers (I had been reading some article about Smith's album Horses just the day before), Makavejev and his films, including WR: *Mysteries of the Organism*, Aleister Crowley, Jack Parsons, and L. Ron Hubbard--all linked in this particular link, all of them names in my own secret pantheon of enthusiasms. And in the midst of it all was a photo of a button with the Steig cartoon. It appears as the article makes reference to one of Reich's dubious achievements: the Orgone Box. I did some more digging.

Turns out Steig credits Reich with "saving his life" through encounters with the emigre analyst in New York in the 1940s. Steig evidently owned an Orgone box and sat in it every day of his life. The angry "chinaman" is, in fact, an image in which Steig is exploring symbolically some aspect of his Reichean experience. Much of his work did.

I'm not a Reichian, but, because of my background in psychoanalysis and my study at the University of West Georgia's Psychology Department (where I perpetually had to temper the temptations to take piercing the veil seriously--the hallways vibrating with it...), I'm intrigued by Reich, and I'm intrigued by others who have been intrigued by Reich, and an image of a large portion of that world of interest was contained in the cartoon in a way that now feels like a marker of destiny. Even here the clash of the *material* and the *non-*. This was not the exercise in autobiography I was expecting.

Further oddness. I clicked on another link…

http://www.kevinislaughter.com/2005/people-are-no-damn-good/

Kind of funny. A collection of "black velvet" work by a Tahitian artist, including a version of the cartoon. Go down to the comments. Someone asks who the original artist was for the cartoon. Kevin Slaughter, whose blog it is, thinks it's Donald Hardman. But he is corrected by someone named "Marc," who identifies the artist as Steig. It was not me. It was some other Marc with a "c."

So I wound up discovering that the cartoon in my father's wallet did, in fact, lead to a very accurate portrait of who I am. It's amazing to me that so many of my interests, and my identity to a certain extent, was, through the cartoon, thrown up onto a screen in an instant. Did someone say "synchronicity?" Why not? I didn't get to the root of myself as a misanthrope stuck in a box, however. I'll have to work more on my own to put that story together.

31

The copies have become indistinct.
Indistinct?
Utterly unreadable.
It might be time.
Time?
To replace your Pinter cartridge.
Yes. I think it might be time.

TUHmult? TOOmult? TUHmult? TOOmult?
TUHmult?
TOOmult?
And in other news, the floors are sweating.

Like those trains hauling freight
out of the Sunshine State
assorted juices
spilling in our cabooses
running too fast
running too late

A Theatre is where you will find Charm under
house arrest and closely monitored.

32

I tap a vein
in my reptile brain.

Sooner or later
you will be introduced to yourself.
And that will be that.

spidery spindly skeletal demons that sport vi-
sors to gain protection from harmful sunlight are
emerging from the shadows and snatching babies all over town then rapidly fleeing down the
sidewalks while trundling their precious captives
in little carts. End times?

Underneath the wiper blade,
a note of explanation.

Experimental theatre is just actors sitting in the
lapse of the audience.

You find the one true calling to which you can be
tirelessly devoted: remove all evidence of your existence.

The decision is getting increasingly difficult to make each morning: today do I
hunt or do I gather?

The research lab was not thoroughly
cleaned--we still found a few rhesus pieces.

composting is difficult even with many words in
your disposal

they walk on water because they're pierless.

it will be hard to stomach another "non-symboliz-
able kernel."

a definition of regret: of all the stuff we sweep
away, only dust returns

trying to breathe in the fumings of his own past-
pyrations leads to a 'snuff vocation

some plastic surgeons offering lip service to eye
deals

A Walk

There on the roadside, at the tempo of impasse,
analyzing the doughy mud of plod,
I squeeze each bit of gravel like a wet grape--
but I do mind my inner parent
and try to look up now and then.

Rewarded with the image of a tall tree,
leaves caught in the rush of wind,
I note "the joy of looking up."
When I get home I'll write it down.

Songs seep like leaks from cracks.

So much misses narration:
the emptying of the road--
travelers alive at a faster particle pace,
breathing into the pulsing future,
vanishing into corpuscular doorways
I'll never see.

Dandelions

A sign someone's chosen to spend more time
in cool curtained rooms.
I see them waggling in yards as I pass.
Folks are tired.
A capitulation's occurred,
a giving up on the Idea,
a giving in to that Lie
as old as the Line:
the belief in some beauty
not bought, some beauty
now free to climb through
since we've set aside the scythe.

"Truth is, we are what we are, and we are what we aren't."

"I am not a Professional Shakespearean Actor, but I play one on TV."

Renewing commitment to finding endings only after making beginnings. The only acceptable use of gerunds, actually.

On creative group performance development

A number of posts and links on this website are devoted to help-ing teach methods to performance groups interested in creat-ing original work. I am trying to reach all manner of groups and performers with all types of experience from high school actors wanting to try something a little different for one-act competition to independent artists searching for new methods. What follows is an introduction to the Vocal Sequence Tutorial page, through which you can access other group development materials on this website.

During some past summers I helped teach Theatre for the Georgia Governor's Honors Program (GHP). We had thirty high-school age kids all to ourselves for five to six weeks and a number of lofty goals: to turn them into a performance group, to introduce them to some collective creation processes, and to inspire them to develop an original performance piece. My contribution to this program was based on what I learned as a graduate directing student at Catholic University from 1987 to 1990 working with Jackson Phippin. And that learning experience was shaped by the work of Herbert Blau and the experimental performance group KRAKEN. Jackson had been a member of KRAKEN. When I began working with him (a number of years after the end of KRAKEN), I was already a disciple of Blau through my reading.

I am not writing about KRAKEN, however. Blau has done that himself in numerous books, speeches, and papers. I am merely attempting to make a record of a few things I learned from Jackson which I think are valuable for performers attempt-ing creative group effort. My own attempts to transmit these things through my work at GHP have always left me somewhat frustrated (in spite of the work of very talented students). And I have wrestled with formulating an explanation. The circum-stances under which I taught at GHP were different from those under which I was taught, and those circumstances were al-ready on the other side of the world from what was going on in KRAKEN. And while I was not foolish enough to think I was trying to re-create KRAKEN at GHP (I didn't try to maintain any kind of rigorous theoretical agenda for one thing), I was trying to re-capture something of the sense of group possibility I experienced working with Jackson. That kind of group growth and creative engagement wasn't happening at GHP in the ways I desired. Trying to do too much with too many who were too young? Too easy an excuse, I think. Was it me and certain insurmountable gaps in my knowledge? In part, yes. But I also keep coming back to the importance of time and the way in which the students get introduced to the material. This leads me to think specifically of the Vocal Sequence, a series of exercises developed by KRAKEN and one of the things transmitted to me by Jackson Phippin.

One of my students this past summer asked me if I would ever consider teaching the Vocal Sequence in a workshop at "Thespian Conference." He went on to tell me that someone had conducted such a workshop previously. He added that the teacher of this workshop had done little more than introduce the elements. Frustrating, yes, but in a one or two-hour workshop how could you do more? And what could be seriously gained? After all, it's just a list of possibilities for vocalizing combined with some Michael Chekov-inspired imaginative structures. It reads on the page like a series of stunts, and the list is out there for any who might want to read it and then make the attempt. To "teach" the Vocal Sequence as an independent thing is really just to facilitate such an attempt. An hour with a roomful of ambitious, eager-to-please and eager-to-entertain students is plenty of time to get something to happen, but it won't have the same scope as what I am usually after.

Teaching and time. I'm trying to find a diminishing orbit into my point. The Vocal Sequence played a particular role in the life and evolution of KRAKEN. As one of Jackson's students I was led into work with the Vocal Sequence as a member of a group, and the methods Jackson used to introduce us to the Sequence were also serving to engender a certain psychological disposition among all of us as performing group members. The Vocal Sequence became for us a way to make a particular kind of creative and existential investment in the mystery in our midst. To undertake the Vocal Sequence was to take an investigative risk and raise the stakes in your relationships with fellow group members. Needless to say, such evolution and learning took time. And there was from the beginning an intrinsic link between learning and the birth of material; we were the stuff from which material sprang as much as from any texts or ideas at play in our work.

In my teaching at GHP I never set this kind of deep evolution into motion in a way which might unleash full creative potential and exchange in the students. Lack of time, of course, is always a factor, but I also think I never did enough in transmitting the Vocal Sequence to link the learning of the Sequence to the immediate possible creation of material. The time spent applying the Vocal Sequence to our group creation always existed separately from the time spent learning the elements. In my own way I was falling prey to the "workshop" mentality of teaching the Sequence. Everything which was bubbling up as the students learned the Sequence should have immediately been woven into a creative group process and an expanding working vocabulary.

Practically speaking, the text you pick to teach the Vocal Sequence needs to be one of the texts you would pick for your performance piece. All learning needs to be situated in the world you want to explore creatively. Otherwise, you waste opportunities for group enrichment and process work.

I have attempted to put together a series of steps for learning the Vocal Sequence suitable for acting students from high-school age on to adults, and I am trying to create an experience for students that is as close as possible to my experience learning from Jackson Phippin, something more ideal in structure than my past GHP efforts. The goal, ideally, is to acquire the Vocal Sequence as a vital element in creative group work, to grow with the Sequence as the group grows. Those of you interested in undertaking this kind of work need to keep that in mind. And keep in mind, also, that I have limited myself in these steps, as in other materials on this site, to providing frameworks only. I try to avoid fabricating examples of content or of dynamic group relationship. Such precious particularity and treacherous depth is waiting to reveal itself to whomever tries this kind of work. Such illustrating is also very difficult and I haven't figured out a way to do it. Blau's *Take Up the Bodies* is still the best source of "illustrations."

a friend abandoning her dream and returning to domestic life: too bored with a Pashtun.

Finally going to buff up, buzz my head, and start scowling. Conformity or camouflage?

lèse-majesté feels like the plan for the day

each of us is composed of a number of tape loops of varying lengths

The Psychoanalytic Performer: an invitation to the unknowing

What does a performer do?

Once we asserted the performer was a Shaman.

Now we will see the performer as a Scientist.

Neither comparison is true…

What are you? An actor, an artist, a performer? A Student? A Shaman? A Scientist?

Not one of these is true…

"They're all true." Perhaps that's true. But as a formulation a bit too tried and true. We'll see…

"Your name here." What are you?

Your name here. That's true. Your head probably turns when you hear it. Hear what? "It" in the previous sentence refers to…

Your name? Performer? "Adolescent?" Artist? Friend? Scientist? Are any of these true?

 What do you do as a performer? What do you do as "Your name here?" Besides turn your head when called…

 Performance Artist. That's a phrase which makes your teacher comfortable.

 Previously: "The Performance Artist is like a Shaman…"

 Now: "The Performance Artist is like a Scientist…"

 Your teacher wants to keep both terms in play because he can't let go of the first to embrace the second exclusively.

 It's fashionable in such a situation to inscribe the slash: /

The slash is not a cut in this case but rather a…conjoining? Interesting. "Both/and…"

 Your teacher pauses at the choice of the word "embrace" in a recent sentence.

 Your teacher wonders about the choice of the word "comfortable" in a recent sentence.

 You ask questions.

Your teacher is characterizing you as someone who asks questions. Is that true?

Your teacher asks questions because not only is he preoccupied with questions–with questions of performance, particularly, at present, and with the performing of questions–but also because he is a student of psychoanalysis.

You might as well know that at the outset. Doesn't mean he's interested in whether or not you are sane. He's trying to find out what psychoanalysis can say about the art of performance.

Psychoanalysis is the study of how we ask and answer questions, among other things.

It also studies how people get from one thing…

To the next.

Note the curious way in which this introduction is composed: words, assertions, identities, questions…

And a pause between one thing and the next.

The pauses are included for your use. No extra charge.

What happens between one thing…

And the next?

> What happens when you are asked a question?
>
> 42   What happens when you read a word?
>
> And when that word is brought into a relationship with another word?

Where are you?

Who's reading?

Speak the word.

And the next…

Who's speaking?

Whose speaking?

There will be more puns. Puns pretend to play while purporting to point.

Who's there nay answer me stand and unfold yourself…A bit of Shakespeare. From the first scene of Hamlet. Shakespeare is surely an example of a writer's words on a page producing many questions in the reader. What's the matter my lord between who what do you read my lord…more Shakespeare.

What about my language? "My" being given special emphasis in the uttering.

"What about my language–Shakespeare doesn't speak to me…"

Word words words…

Consider the word "uttering." Strange word. Makes your teacher think "uddering." Milking…Something performers know about.

Your teacher wants to reassure you about this not being a Shakespeare seminar but also wants to avoid absolutes. On this occasion.

No one is ever speaking to you.

Pause.

Bold assertion, that. True? Surely not true. But…Are there ways in which it might be true?

Another assertion: The actor cannot take speaking at face value.

When you speak in a performance you try to summon something very particular and powerful, don't you? Memorable, even? How? And what makes you so memorable and powerful and meaningful?

Full of meaning…Uttering…Milking…

James Cagney: "Just look the other fellow in the eye and tell the truth."

We want to agree because we revere James Cagney, but…

"look"("the eye") +"tell"(ears to hear?)(mouths of babes?)+"other"="the truth"

Complex equation, that. What are we agreeing to do?

From now on to the end what you will be reading is a Laboratory Manual for the Experimenting Performance Artist. In it you will find some fundamental structures to use as a foundation for creating new theatre performance possibilities. The next century belongs to the geneticists, they say, so think of yourself as a scientist growing new life forms in a Petri dish. Also included in the manual are exercises created from the fundamental structures, to give you illustrations of how to move ahead. Also included are the un-exorcizable spirits of shamans from an earlier time. They haunt some of the words. They rest in some of the pauses. May they help guide you in moments when science is silent.

Common factor: both scientists and shamans have found ways to negotiate with chthonic entities.

The most difficult lesson a writer must learn is what to leave out. With diligence, practice, and years of perseverance, you eventually achieve a level of mastery where you need hardly write anything at all. You finally understand that the power of the written word resides not in your effort but in the reception of the reader. You accept that, ultimately, the imaginary land of enchantment you are seeking to chart through creative effort lies wholly upon the shimmering peaks and within the shadowy valleys of the reader's cortex. It is the reader who does the work and unearths the prize and who, when all is done, achieves treasured transformation. The writer should merely provide occasional gestures of guidance or a smile of encouragement now and then. My current work method is as follows: I set an empty sheet on the table before me. I stare at the blank surface for five to ten minutes at a stretch depending on the time of day and my level of alertness. Then I turn the sheet over to appreciate how the reverse side is equally as blank. However, it is far more than a flip of the sheet--it is a momentous act, one I accomplish slowly and reverently. By turning it over, I have signified that I *turn over* the task of creativity to the reader. My work is done. I look ahead to the beginning of my next project. As an artist, I have reached a point where all I have to do is clear my throat and the audience will begin singing. That is as it should be.

Yard Sale

Those nights you let me peel thoughts from your shoulders.

The gown with its spectral splitting of moon.

Loomed with the adventurous thread

only an exuberant wartime chemistry could extrude.

Knowing it was your mother's

made the night silly and obscene,

the dance paralyzing and enticing.

We kept it in a dark stained drawer of wonder

eddying and swirling, gestating, waiting.

They inspect it and me.

How much do I want for it?

Our sunglasses locked in combat. I'm outmatched.

And how much for you, they might as well ask.

I never leave my lawn chair.

It's stretched out on a hanger now,

45

baked flat and dry by a Saturday morning,

as blunt and embarrassing as an out-of-date anatomical chart.

Clearly lacking the latest information. Quaint.

Setting an antique tone.

Should I tell the story behind it

or let it speak for itself?

In the end I pretty much give it away.

The Vocal Sequence: a tutorial

(This tutorial was written as a response to a request from a friend who worked at the time for the Georgia Department of Education. She was developing online instructional modules and asked me if I would consider creating a course conveying what I taught for the Governor's Honors Program. You will note the ingenuous, transparent, and consistently encouraging tone. It's a series of steps anyone can follow. Anyone. I wanted the teacher to feel capable and empowered and, perhaps most importantly, assured that what's on offer is legitimate knowledge. Nothing sketchy. Canonical theatre education. At no point do I discuss the possible visitations from monsters or demons or of opening doors for extra-dimensional entities of eldritch aspect. We reject the naysayers. No need to fear arts education in the schools. Was my approach a touch irresponsible?)

STEP: 1

46

The students should get some idea of what is to come and what the Vocal Sequence is. Tell them they will soon be given a detailed description of a performance exercise which they will learn to master. It's called the Vocal Sequence. It builds confidence and power and inspires new kinds of creativity. It is an example of the kind of concerns theatre artists were pursuing in the late Sixties and early Seventies. Inspired by Brook, Grotowski, Chaikin, a host of other artists, and by the writings of Artaud, theatre artists were exploring the most extreme possibilities for performance, tapping into the actor's expressive resources in new ways. One practical result of this was the development of new possibilities for exploiting the actor's voice and body in performance. New exercises and systems emerged. The Vocal Sequence was compiled by pioneer American director and theorist Herbert Blau in collaboration with his experimental group KRAKEN. It is a series of activities which actors do all the time—involving the body and speaking text, for warm-up, relaxation, exploration, play, and practice—charted into a map for performance.

STEP: 2

Text. To work with he Vocal Sequence you need text. The students must memorize "The Sick Rose" by William Blake as soon as possible. (You can find the poem at the end of The Vocal Sequence, another file available on the *lacunagroup* site.) Other texts or poems can be used for teaching purposes. Requirements: the material should be rich in imagery, the words must allow for a variety of vocalizing possibilities, and the material should be short enough for quick memorization. This is your sole text for the duration of training, so it requires a certain depth of expression, perhaps a touch of riddling difficulty. And part of training involves learning to use the Vocal Sequence to discover material for performance pieces, so your text needs to be something you are willing to explore in that way.

STEP: 3

Breathing. Tell the students the key to learning the Vocal Sequence is to understand the following: "If you are breathing, you are speaking." If they apply this rule always, they will discover how the Sequence is supposed to feel when executed. Use the method illustrated in the following to lead the students toward beginning to master proper vocal technique (the observations in what follows have not been confirmed by a physiologist or speech pathologist; they are merely offered as aids to visualization and new body awareness):

You will be speaking and breathing and exerting yourselves physically. You need to know how to breathe properly to protect your voice. The values for this are basically the same as those taught by voice teachers. If you have been working with voice teachers, you are encouraged to share the methods of visualization you have been taught previously to enhance the following suggestions.

47

The throat and the shoulders and the chest area must remain relaxed. The source of energy for sound is not produced there, and tightening or constricting those muscles through throat clenching or chest heaving is counter-productive and harmful. Such exertion leads to laryngitis, among other things. The belly is what breathes. You can place your hands on your tummy and experience the motion of the diaphragm as it expands and contracts, pushing air the way a bellows does. The chest and throat do not labor; they merely provide, along with the skull, a series of resonating chambers. As air is pushed by the diaphragm through the throat, the vocal cords are set to vibrating. The more relaxed the throat and the cords, the more colorful and rich are these initial vibrating frequencies. The chest, the belly, the throat, and the mouth all work as resonating and amplifying media for the sound vibrations issuing from the vocal cords.

(When developing vocal warm-ups for the students, make sure you provide them opportunities to work sound in all the resonating cavities of the body.)

Every approach to breathing and vocalizing involves some form of visualization. Try using a balloon. Blow up a balloon. You can liken the elastic nature of the balloon to the elastic nature of the diaphragm. The muscles stretch as air is pulled into the body. Like the material of the balloon, the stretched diaphragm contains potential energy which is soon to be transmitted into vocal energy. Pull taut the opening of the balloon, release air, and create that wonderful squealing and whining tone. The stretched rubber opening vibrates as the air escapes and the vibration is transmitted to the molecules of the air. Our ears process this disturbance as sound. The stretched elastic balloon opening vibrates just as the stretched elastic tissues of the vocal cords vibrate when

48 air escapes the body. In fact, if you could somehow record the sound of vibrating vocal cords outside of the body's complex resonating container, the sound would resemble the wheeze of the deflating balloon.

How can you make a balloon deflate faster? By squeezing it, of course. But it depends on how you squeeze the balloon. If you squeeze near the opening, you may get some air to push out faster, but then...you choke off the balloon and most of the air is still inside. This kind of squeezing is akin to an attempt to strain with the chest and neck to gain vocal power. Most of the air stays in the body and/or you wind up closing down the resonating potential of those areas, and you are left using your throat muscles to yank around the vocal cords. To get the most out of your balloon, you need to push from underneath. The outlet is unimpeded. You apply pressure, but the elastic contracting chamber is still working at maximum potential in addition to whatever extra pressure you apply. Blow up the balloon, stretch the opening to create sound with the escaping air, and push the bottom of the balloon against the tummy to add pressure to the escaping air. Try exhaling with the balloon. Then blow up the balloon again, and then inhale this time not by expanding the lungs but by pushing down and out with your tummy muscles (in fact your tummy should poke out a bit, a distressing state of affairs for the body-conscious teenager, but there you are...). Now push the bottom of the balloon against your "activated" tummy as you release air and make the whining sound. You should exhale slowly as the balloon "exhales" and continue to apply tummy pressure to the bottom of the balloon. This complicated exercise is designed to lead you to experience the great paradox of supported vocal production: when you take in air, you expand the diaphragm, pushing the tummy out as you tighten the abdominal muscles, then as you exhale, you keep pushing down and out with the tightened tummy.

This balloon illustration emphasizes that the diaphragm is the only muscle mass doing work during vocalizing—everything else should be relaxed and open and employed for resonance and amplification, and engaging the muscles of the diaphragm increases its general elasticity during the inhale and the exhale; greater elasticity means more potential energy; the result is more strength and more capacity in the use of air (greater capacity for volume and duration).

Belly breathing and support not only improves vocalization; it is what allows a performer to vocalize while doing other demanding things such as dancing. In other words, the belly takes care of the breathing while the rest of the body can exert itself in other ways. And as the rate of respiration increases during activity, vocal support stays in place. When performing the Vocal Sequence, it is essential to breath this way since you are to follow the dictum "if you are breathing you are speaking." You don't get to "catch your breath" and then continue. And once the body is fully involved, the process gets more demanding.

STEP: 4

Observation and mirroring. The students are to maintain a journal which they will use to record observations and reflections in class after exercises and between classes in preparation for upcoming lessons. Eventually this journal will also be useful for remembering and developing material created using the Vocal Sequence. Students should spend some time writing after most exercises, beginning with the "mirror what you see" described next.

Mirroring. Students divide into pairs and sit facing their partners. Tell them they will do a mirror exercise. After the groaning has subsided, you ask the pairs, both partners, to sit quietly and "mirror what you see." There will be questions; try not to waste too much time with answers. The exercise leads to something of a paradox: how can both partners mirror without one leading the other? This is the interesting aspect. How will the students negotiate this predicament? You respond to all reservations with "just mirror what you see…" Give them five to ten minutes and then ask them to write a description of their experience in their journals, including all thoughts and imaginings which occurred. Take time for some discussion. As a way to punctuate the discussion, you might mention that the possibility of "becoming absorbed in the other" was one idea the exercise was introducing. This capacity to "become absorbed" and have it lead to focused imaginative activity is crucial for executing the Vocal Sequence. Then add that this mirroring approach will be one chief way of transmitting information both vocal and physical in the days ahead. Some of the more thoughtful students might also be intrigued by this idea: if you are truly mirroring your partner and if your partner is truly mirroring what he or she sees, then you are in fact seeing your own unconscious self in your partner's efforts and taking that unconscious self upon your own self as Other.

50

STEP: 5

"Come up from silence and return to silence." All Vocal Sequence work is framed by this convention. Here's a way to introduce the idea. Students lie comfortably on their backs. You invite them to breathe with their bellies in the manner previously discussed. As they begin breathing you ask them to think of the phrase "Hah-Yah." Tell them to begin thinking the phrase as they breathe and as if they were speaking it. The phrase can be imagined as short punctuations or long vowel extensions. (The "hahs" activate the diaphragm and then allow for vowel extension; the "yahs" offer access to the "y-buzz" of Lessac fame and then an extension.) Encourage them to try both ways and note how they require and engender different breathing. Remind them to breathe with their bellies. Now invite them to bring the phrase into their breath as a whisper, without letting the vocal cords vibrate. Then tell them that on your cue they will go from

whispering to barely vocalizing the phrase and then gradually increase volume until they reach "normal speaking volume." Once that is achieved, they will begin to gradually increase volume as they explore the phrase, by slowing it down, speeding it up, emphasizing different aspects, etc, and ultimately they should reach what they consider maximum volume. Continue proper breathing. Having achieved maximum volume, they should begin to reduce volume, returning finally to "normal speaking" and then to the barely audible and then to whisper and finally to silently hearing the phrase "in their heads." Encourage them to take all the time they need to complete the cycle and cue them to "go." Afterwards, allow time for writing and discussion. How did what they felt and heard influence their own explorations? Remind them that all work will "come up from silence and return to silence" in a manner similar to what they have just undertaken.

STEP: 6

Mirroring with the voice is another interesting impossibility for the students to attempt. Pair them off as in the previous mirroring introduction (rotation of partners is advised to help build trust and group cohesiveness). Both partners are to begin breathing and then to think the phrase "Hah-Yah." Bring the phrase to breath and then to voice as in the "come up from silence and return to silence" exercise in the previous step. However, as they both do this, they are both to "mirror what they see and hear." In other words, as they come up from silence, they should stay absorbed in one another, both partners attempting to breathe and vocalize as one, producing the same rhythm, sound, texture, intonation, pitch, etc. Encourage the students to proceed slowly, giving each student plenty of time to match what they experience in the other and to change with it. The "goal" is for an observer not to be able to detect a gap in response between partners as the vocalizing proceeds. They should gradually proceed to "normal speech" and then let the vocal impulse change, very gradually, expanding in volume and varying in rate of repetition, varying also in vowel duration. Keep in mind the rule of thumb "if you're breathing, you're speaking." Their vocal engagement should be continuous; a gradually evolving rhythmic pulse is inevitable. Reach a maximum limit and slowly return to silent breath, "mirroring" all the way. Write and discuss. In discussion, encourage colorful impressionistic language from the students. Help them uncover new metaphors for describing their experiences. Remember, every exercise is as much an experience for the student as it is a moment of instruction.

51

Students need to take time after each exercise to record their experience in their journals and to discuss their experiences in terms of challenges, discoveries and imaginative reverie.

STEP: 7

On to the next mirror exercise. Change partners. Give them the word "one." Breathe together and then come up from silence with the word "one," each partner mirroring the other carefully (not specifying a leader and follower in these exercises encourages a more thoughtful and sober engagement with the processes of absorption and observation, every emotion tends to be more "real," every idea more provocative). Once normal speech is reached, students can begin to note how the body seems to participate in the vocalizing. Let a physical idea become a part of what is vocalized; let it emerge, rhythmically develop, and gradually change along with the vocal exploration. Mirror what you see and hear as closely as you can. Take it to a limit and gradually bring it back. Reflect and write. The ideal is a mirroring link where voice and body impulses seem to emerge and evolve as..."one." You cannot tell the "dancer from the dance." If the teacher sees a pair of students who accomplish a particularly unified exploration, the pair should attempt to "recapitulate" it for the class.

52

STEP: 8

Tell the students "The Sick Rose" will definitely have to be memorized by the next meeting. End the present session with Quick Pass. Have them stand in a circle, mats (yes, there should be mats) and plenty of space in their midst. Invite one student to come to the center of the circle. (This will be a variation on a familiar impulse exercise to many.) The student should breathe and come up from silence with the phrase "Hah-Yah," Every student in the circle should attempt to mirror the student in the middle. Once the student in the middle has reached normal speech, he or she should attach a physical component to the vocalizing. Then let the sound and image impulse take on a definite repeating pulse. Let it change and develop in the repeating pulsation. "If you're breathing, you're speaking" and the body is now perpetually involved as well. All students should attempt to mirror the voice and body of the one in the middle. The student in the middle should arrive at some vocal and physical impulse which "pleases" and which can be rhythmically repeated accurately and distinctly by the group. The student, as he or she continues to perform the impulse, must examine the work of the group to assure that everyone is working hard to mirror what they see and hear exactly. Once the student is satisfied with everyone's efforts, s/he picks one student in the circle to "pass" leadership to by going to that student with the rhythmic impulse, establishing a tight mirroring, and switching places with that student who then carries the impulse to the center... The new leader allows the impulse to change, gradually, not abruptly, not arbitrarily, and the group follows. The new leader inspects and passes to a new leader. And so on. The goal is to effect a "quick pass" in which a leader evolves an impulse... impulsively, without thinking about it, and links smoothly and rapidly to a new leader. When the teacher decides the mayhem has gone on long enough, the existing leader can be told to go to silence slowly. In discussion, point out to the students those moments where voice and body inevitably gave birth to emotional, behavioral and imaginative dimensions. Suggest to them they view this activity as a kind of performed imaginative thinking in which, paradoxically, the goal is not to think so much. Follow the impulse.

STEP: 9

By this step the students are to know "The Sick Rose" by William Blake. They will "know" it, but not know it (some, of course, will not yet know it all the way through in any sense). The words need to get into their muscle memory so they will not have to think to speak.

Have them stand in a close circle. Tell them they shall speak the poem as a group with each student speaking one word at a time, around the circle, next student, next word. Keep starting the poem with different students. This round will be a struggle at first as many discover what they don't really remember. The goal is to have the poem flow through the group with no forgetful pauses, with everyone listening and poised to move the text along. Once this goal is reached, the next hurdle is to speak the text person to person, word to word, so that it sounds like one speaker delivering the poem. To do this, students will have to listen attentively and learn to layer the words, overlapping slightly, achieving a uniformity of tone. This entire exercise they will find singularly frustrating.

STEP: 10

Arrange the mats end to end. Students are to roll (sideways, not somersaulting) over the mats as they speak the text, remembering the rule of thumb "if you are breathing, you are speaking." Tell them to use their speaking to give them different kinds of energy for rolling. Fast and slow. Light and labored.

Let the "oomph" of the body become one with the speaking of the words. Do the students want to latch on to certain phrases and repeat them? Encourage them to do so. The idea behind this activity is simply that speaking should become fused with every kind of physical exertion. The exertion should color the speaking and the speaking color the exertion. Students must abandon the tight grip they try to maintain on proper "upright" sounding and speaking. Every twist of a tendon and turn of a bone should be wrapped in the sound of speech and lead to all manner of distortions.

STEP: 11

Invite each student to perform the poem for the class. Each student will attempt to make the poem "meaningful," perhaps by choosing a character who will speak the poem, or by bringing some kind of emotional tone or color to it, or by clowning with it, being "ironic" perhaps. Some may actually be quite accomplished and possess an already impressive bag of tricks from which they pull to achieve a memorable effect. You should let them perform without comment. In a concluding discussion, you can ask about how the students experienced being asked to "perform" the poem. Was there a struggle to determine and then communicate meaning? What was there a goal in the performance? As a way to end discussion, offer the following: "You can stop worrying about the text as a piece of meaningful poetry and about the actor's duty to communicate a meaningful performance which illuminates the literature. Oral interpretation is not required. For you, as you learn the Vocal Sequence, speaking itself is the event; you are a sounding and expressive body, that is the extraordinary phenomenon you will unlock. Think of the text as meaning-less, as simply an opportunity to vocalize." And before they can think about it too much, move to a new variation on Quick Pass...

STEP: 12

In this variation on Quick Pass the first leader will begin speaking "The Sick Rose" silently and then gradually come to normal speech. Everyone should mirror this process exactly (one reason why it is crucial for everyone to learn the poem). Once at normal volume, the leader should let the speaking slooooooow down. All mirror this process. As the leader slows, the body should be brought into the experience of speaking, and the leader should begin to search for some aspect of the bodily sounding which "pleases" or is of interest. This must be done slowly and carefully so the group can mirror as precisely as possible. The leader transforms the discovery into a repeating impulse, a unity of voice, body, and imagination, and more than likely it will have derived from some bit of the text which gets repeated or from a few choice sounds. The leader can explore whatever pleases and affords bodily participation. It should just emerge from repetition and evolution. Once an impulse emerges the leader can vary elements of rate and volume and texture…gradually enough for the group mirroring to stay with it. Quick Pass proceeds as usual; once a new leader takes up the impulse, the leader can move into exploring more of the text before generating a new impulse. Just remember to bring the rest of the group along. Some students may want to preserve the integrity of the poem, its order and sense, at all costs. Encourage everyone to relax and let the text "fall apart." Part of the enjoyment comes with repetitions and juxtapositions of textual fragments.

STEP: 13

The following exercise will help students begin to find the rhythmic life of the Vocal Sequence and to understand how to use the Sequence to make creative discoveries. Divide up into pairs. One partner is to begin reciting "The Sick Rose" silently and then come up from silence and move toward normal speech. The other partner should mirror this process carefully. The first partner should then move speaking into "slow motion" and allow the body to get involved, working gradually enough for the mirroring partner to stay with the activity. Also, re-emphasize the importance of the "if you're breathing, you're speaking" rule of thumb for this exercise. The breath cycle will begin to shape the rhythm to a certain extent. Within this state of "slow motion," tell the first partner to "find something interesting, isolate it, and repeat it." The mirroring partner is to stay with it all the way. This compels the first partner to be accountable to the other partner's efforts. Tell the first partner to allow the repetition of this interesting found artifact to incrementally change it; let it evolve, develop, intensify, diminish, vary in rate, move through various imaginative modes of expression. Emphasize the importance of following the impulse and not imposing changes or "clever" variations. Give the second partner time to sync up with the changes. After about 10 minutes in such a feedback loop, call for a slow return to silence. Then repeat the process with the second partner taking the lead.

Students should be given time to reflect upon this experience and record some observations in their journals. Begin a discussion by asking for "observations…" Another fruitful frame-work can be established by asking "What did you see or hear?" You want to encourage a link among the body/voice impulse, the capacity for imaginative visualization, and the emotional dimension. Encourage attempts to develop storytelling ideas. Ask about their experience with the text. What insights which were discovered while out on the excursion might be brought back to the text? Yet again, emphasize that the students are free to leave "meaning" behind as they explore. The text, after all, will be broken up into fragments as they isolate discoveries. Tell them to embrace the possibility of nonsense. Their most interesting discoveries may be made between the words at this point. Offer the following:

As you go into "slow motion" with the text and in-volve your body in the speaking, the very act of sounding in an unusual way is to be experienced as exciting and inspiring. To make a discovery means to be captivated by some particular way of speaking or sounding which intertwines with some distinctive physical idea. Herbert Blau might call this a very ba-sic instance of "blooded thought." Here is a moment of something performed being regarded as an "idea" which can be subjected to imagi-native variations, linked, etc.

56

If there were students in the preceding exercise who demonstrated a more instinctive ability to isolate "ideas" and then gradually elaborate upon them, you should invite them to demonstrate for the class. "Recapitulate" is a useful word at this point. Tell them: "I noted something interesting you did; it was as if (and then offer a descriptive image)…Could you and your partner come up from silence and try to get back to that?"

STEP: 14

Shift gears now. Have everyone lie on their backs. Tell them: "Lets improvise a vocal score using 'The Sick Rose' as the text. You will begin as usual, silently, and then at your own indi-vidual rate, come to normal voice. Then try to use your speak-ing to create some kind of atmosphere; it can be a psychologi-cal atmosphere or a mood, or it could be an attempt to shape the physical atmosphere in the room. And as always, keep the breathing and sounding going. Discover something as you ex-plore atmosphere, just with your voice this time, and begin to let it evolve or intensify or shift. Fragment and distort at will. Improvise with what you may hear from your fellow perform-ers. Leave behind linear storytelling or oral interpretation and strive for a sublime and powerful musical experience. Listen to what's going on around you and try to create your place in the composition. To conclude, you decide when your part in the composition has reached its 'culmination' and find a way to bring yourself back to silence."

Once the piece has been performed, give time for reflection, writing and discussion. Try to name the piece.

STEP: 15

It is time to introduce the students to a formal description of the Vocal Sequence. Distribute copies of Blau's description which you can find as a file at the *lacunagroup* site. It is taken from a speech, "The Grail of the Voice," which appears in a collection of speeches and essays entitled *The Dubious Spectacle: extremities of theatre 1976-2000* (Blau has graciously permitted my use of his article in teaching The Vocal Sequence). The class should work through the description, reading and discussing collectively in whatever manner you, as teacher, prefer. Tell them they will begin to explore the steps of the Sequence. The ultimate goal is for each of them to execute the first twelve steps of the Sequence as a solo improvisatory performance for their fellow students (limiting it to the first twelve will seem, it is hoped, less intimidating). Once the students have mastered the Sequence in solo performance, they can begin to experiment with using it as a tool to explore scripts, characters, scenes, and more elusive experimental possibilities. They will explore the steps in the Sequence systematically with a partner in the manner introduced earlier, with one partner exploring impulses and the other mirroring, then switching. Point out to them that they already know the first three steps and in their recent exploring may have already touched upon most of the others. In the work to come invite them to keep in mind the following:

STEPS FOR EXPLORING ELEMENTS:

With your partner mirroring you carefully, move through the first three steps of the Sequence; your body should be involved by Slow Motion.

From Slow Motion move to the step to be investigated and explore the speech and body implications, altering as impulse dictates. Do not impose changes.

Find something interesting in your investigation which you will then isolate and repeat, allowing for evolution. Your partner is still mirroring.

Return to the step you've been investigating, then return to Slow Motion, then Normal, then Silence.

Repeat, this time with you mirroring your partner's exploration. And remember, mirror carefully and accurately; if you're breathing, you're speaking.

Sitting or Standing? Explorations can begin from a sitting or standing position. Should you stay seated throughout? Keep in mind the mats are there for a reason. Full body participation is the goal; you should stretch physical possibilities as you stretch the vocal. Use your impulse to get you from sitting to somewhere else or from an upright posture to an uproarious imposture. Try to countenance the laws of gravity in new and challenging ways as your impulses evolve. No limits at this point.

Combining elements. After working through some of the individual elements in the Sequence, students can string a few together in their explorations. Many of the elements can function as natural climaxes in the work (such as duration or faster and faster) and other elements can serve performers before and after such an event, or they can imbed elements within elements (such as expand and contract within create an atmosphere). In any attempt, students should remember that beyond the exercising of speech the additional goal is to let the work lead them to unexpected discoveries. Remind them (repeatedly) to take time in their Sequence work to explore any new discoveries before moving on to other elements. These new discoveries will function as material for further development.

58

STEP: 16

Some work with the Sequence as a "fun" way to end a session. Sit in a large circle at the outer edges of the mats. A set of partners from the day's work is invited to the center. Each partner is to come up from silence using the poem and move into Slow Motion and then into another step each partner may choose. THE PARTNERS DO THIS CONCURRENTLY AND SEPARATELY–NOT MIRRORING THIS TIME. Tell the partners: "Once you have made an interesting discovery, go encounter the Other. And remember, if you're breathing, you're speaking". The goal is for each partner to embody physically and vocally an interesting impulse and then to have it become an "identity" or "entity" which must relate to some other thing. This may play out at the level of "characterization." Or it may take shape as something far more elusive and provocative. Call

for a return to silence, eventually. End with the observing students, one by one, performing a round of: "I saw _____"
(could be an image, an idea, a quote from the text, something else; keep it short, precise or pointedly enigmatic, and…resonant). Move to a new set of partners.

STEP: 17

In order to perform the twelve elements solo, the students need to become comfortable working alone with the elements. At first it works well for each student to have an opportunity to string the elements together without the pressure of an audience (and one goal is for the student to regard the Sequence as a way an actor can work alone on assorted material or work alone simply "playing scales"). Let the students distribute themselves about the space. They are to work concurrently and alone. Instruct them to come up from silence with "The Sick Rose" and systematically move through all twelve elements of the Vocal Sequence. Return to silence when finished. Allow time for writing, reflection, and discussion. Go over the following list of standards for performance:

Questions to ask yourself when performing The Vocal Sequence:

Am I speaking when breathing? Is it perpetual? 59
Am I breathing properly from the belly?

Did I begin by speaking silently? Then move to normal?

Is my body involved fully?

Did I make a conscious decision to move to each element? Did I cover all the elements? Do I know all the elements?

Am I finding and maintaining impulse rhythms as I move through the elements?

Am I following the sound, the act of speaking? Have I stopped trying to impose meaning?

Did I give myself an opportunity to make a discovery while engaged with each element? Did I fully use the element as a stepping off point for investigation before moving on to the next element?

Am I staying open and ready for all emotional and imaginative experience?

Is my transition to the next element fluid?

Was I fully absorbed in the process? Did concentration and attention free me from self-awareness? Did I accept and welcome the audience's attention without pandering to it?

Did I allow myself to be surprised?

Note: The first three steps of the Sequence should always come first; Slow Motion is a great one for getting the body involved. Practice the steps in the printed order until you know them well; after that any order can be interesting. And you can move back and forth among the elements freely, returning to any as you wish, using silence and normal at any tune. Use a *lite* approach to the Sequence to accomplish physical and vocal warm-ups. Voice and body should always work in partnership, even when stretching muscles.

STEP: 18

Take a break from the solo work and have some more fun with group improvisation. Available at the *lacunagroup* website are descriptions of *Breakout/Breakdown (Breaking Away)* and *Hysterical Hygeneassist,* two formats for improvisation taken from the GHP experimental theatre manual. *Breakout* is a specific dimension of Vocal Sequence work in which a performer takes a discovery and transforms it into a realistic characterization; *Hysterical Hygeneassist* is an interesting improv game which can also be employed with *Breakout*. Students can use "The Sick Rose" as the text.

60

STEP: 19

Students are almost ready to undertake their solo improvisations. A last preparation will involve performing some elements of the Sequence for an audience. Circle up and use some Quick Pass to warm up. "The Sick Rose" continues to be the text. Let the students know ahead of time that at your word, after a certain amount of time in Quick Pass, a leader will stay in the center and the rest of the group will sit in their circle. The leader will take his or her impulse and move it specifically into an element in the Sequence (a new element), explore it, perhaps make a discovery, and then pursue yet another new element. After three elements, the student will find a watcher in the circle, transfer the impulse to that watcher through a mirror (the rest of the group is just watching, not constantly mirroring), and the new student will explore three elements. Then pass it on. And so on. Allow time for writing and discussion afterwards.

This is also an opportune moment to explore more explicitly how Vocal Sequence explorations can be used in group-driven creative process leading at some point to the development of an original performance piece. It might be useful to introduce the structure Show/Reflect/Recapitulate, illustrated elsewhere on the *lacunagroup* site, as a possible way to work with material. The period during which everyone performs their elements and then passes to the next performer can be considered the Show period. It proceeds without comment or interruption this time and the next few times this structure is attempted.

(Soon, however, once the execution of Vocal Sequence work in this set-up becomes easy and un-self-conscious, it will be crucial to begin inviting students to involve themselves in one another's explorations. The material on Show/Reflect/Recapitulate offers many ideas, but to get things started, go to students who are watching a peer work and tell them to try things. Tell a student to go in and mirror what the performing student is doing; invite a number of students to mirror simultaneously. Invite a student to simply "encounter" the performing student. Instruct a student to offer a "description" of what is being performed. Ask a student to attempt to "read" a performance the way an oracle might read some particular sign. Make these suggestions quietly, without breaking the concentration of the Vocal Sequence performer. Once the students are finished involving themselves in the performance, they should simply return to their place in the circle and the work should continue.)

After everyone has been in the center and worked through their elements, they should make their own notes in their journals about what happened. This is the Reflect period. You can encourage them to feel free to write in any way about their experience as a performer and as an audience member. Encourage them to write with the poem as a frame of reference if they wish. You can begin to invite them explicitly to think about the possibilities for a performance piece based on what is happening in the circle.

The best way to introduce the idea of the Recapitulation stage is to encourage the students to ask to "see things again." There need be no desire to comment upon the event or to change it or "stage" it in some way (though all of that is certainly possible). You want the students to understand how crucial their memories are in keeping the creative process alive. If they wish, as they are witnessing that which they asked their peers to "recapitulate," they may share reflections or observations or ask provoking questions. They may open the event up for further exploration through performance. As the teacher, you should be prepared to play a number of roles at this point. As director, you might think out loud about possible future avenues of investigation; as designer, you might discuss images or make visual associations; as writer, you might note implications for the understanding of the poem or new possibilities of text, of "dialogue" or choral possibilities. The students should understand that a performance piece derived from Blake's "The Sick Rose" has already begun to evolve and reveal itself.

STEP: 20

Performing the Sequence solo. The group will undertake this in a ritualized manner. Circle up, seated around the mats. A volunteer moves to the center and comes up from silence, beginning the Sequence with "The Sick Rose" (Students must avoid using the popular variation called "Sick of the Sick Rose"). The first twelve elements are to be explored; the transitions should be distinct. When the student feels he or she is done, s/he returns to Slow Motion, and if elements have been overlooked, a group member should call out the missing elements. The student can then move from Slow Motion back to work with the overlooked elements. Return to silence when finished. The performing student remains quietly in the center while the circle of watchers undertakes a round of "I saw _____," as described in a previous step. The performer leaves the center and a new volunteer moves in and begins. Encourage those who have performed to take some time to jot down any crucial sensations or discoveries immediately after performing and before giving their attention to the next performer.

62

STEP: 21

Students will be crying out for other opportunities to use the Sequence. The article *The Real Thing* contains some suggestions for using the Vocal Sequence in scene preparation. A male actor, a female actor, and a student director could undertake the exercise as a working group. Possible scripts are included in the article. Have several groups working concurrently over a period of time; then have a "scene showcase." Students should be intrigued by what will inevitably be a series of variations on familiar material.

WARNING: The scenes, from the work of Molnar, have been chosen for their charm and ambiguity. They both depict romantic communication between a male and a female. One scene refers to a character's past experience with implied physical intimacy and employs an ironic use of the word "prostitute." By all means, consider the age and maturity of your students, and feel free to substitute other scenes which depict difficult relationships among characters with a modicum of wit and theatrical charm.

STEP: 22

"The Sick Rose"–a performance piece. Why not? By this point, the group could easily position itself to work out an event which unfolds myriad riches contained in the text and in their experiences as performers with the text. You could create a performance which composes a grand recapitulation of memories, jottings, extra research on Blake, certain motifs which have repeated among the students. The Vocal Sequence will simply be one possibility for exploration within the undertaking (*Viewpoints* is also a useful tool, see Anne Bogart and Tina Landau's book). The group has a "history" already in place in reference to the text; they can begin to make some of that history explicit and attach meanings to it. Call it a treasury of sub-text ready to be explored.

The main thing the students need to begin to appreciate as they gather each time in their working circle is that apart from the text(s) they are using and the research they have done, the chief material which will lead to the final piece is themselves, their personal experiences working in the circle, their history in the group, and their relationships with their fellow performers. All of it becomes part of the meanings at play in the final work.

63

The text has been with them from the beginning, from their first attempts to learn the Vocal Sequence and understand group creative process. It is contained in the sediment of their history and colors their own private group vocabulary. Their relationship to it is primordial and intimate, and it is that relationship to the text which must inform the continuing work and the final result.

The *Cat She Did* Collection

Cat she did catch a katydid.

Cat she reaches with screeching catachresis.

Cat she gags playing hair catarrh.

Cat she spies a new specimen to categorize.

Cat she yowls catastrophic vowels.

Cat she loves gin till she's catatonic. (courtesy of Sue Mc-Cully)

Cat she love cataloging.

Cat she hissed a tryst catalyst.

Cat she leapt till cataleptic.

Cat she tries to catechize us on her dinner's size.

"Cat she fought" carved on her catafalque.

Cat she licks her fur with inexhaustible catalytic conversion.

Cat she moans and roams through catacombs.

Cat she catches and coaches chipmunks and roaches.

Cat she walks the wall swallowing a caterwauling swallow.

Cat she has sat on the hazmat: a cataclysm!

Cat she changes her name to Cat Stevens.

Cat she is wary when I put on Katy Perry.

Cat she can't: she's Catholic.

Cat she stammers jibes and ribs when I reference the Katzenjammer Kids.

Cat she inserts a claw catheter through my shorts--yes, it hurts.

Cat she killed them last month in the Catskills.

Cat she stalks Kate in the Bush.

Cat she don't in Katmandu: so she broods, mews and stews over veggie brews.

Cat she's old but beams like a cathode.

Cat she can counteract the cataracts with contacts.

Cat she bats at flies and caterpillars.

Cat she tore, *zut alors*, through *les petits fours: pas douze, pas treize, mais voilà, quatorze.*

has no element to be out of

depend is deepened with a mere shift of emphasis

Sunday School! Frankfurt School!

feels the tense in pretense...puts the
tense in pretense

"Baritones cannot truly possess either Air
or Earth; instead they leap among a few peaks,
brandishing a Promethean torch, trying to keep it
lit. The voice confesses the fear that the flame will
soon extinguish. And it does."

Workshops and Seminars? Save your money. All
you need to know is that if you enjoyed writing it,
you need to prune.

Have. Had. Will Have Had. Grammar: the low-cost
psychotropic.

Waxing Talmudic these days.

Hymn to willows

My first and only decree shall be:
A willow in every yard!
The teddy bear of trees are these.
Who knew such life could droop
and not provoke a peep of complaint.
Send those burr-head little monsters
on a rampage round one some time
and watch the crenelated shade
dissolve all malevolence.
Laboring neighbors plop down
against the slender trunk--
instant brotherhood of man!
A cool hold on us it has,
a caress from the tree of truth--
brushing branches,
Asclepian serpents,
brash boas of light.
Every house grows feathered wings
and lifts into the blue.

Sun Room

Finally put in that sun room.

She's been asking for it forever.

Closed in the swing porch.

Nice young fella did the work. Took his time.

His wife just had a baby girl.

Every day he showed us new pictures.

The room's got so much glass.

We walk some mornings

while it's still cool.

Coming up the last hill you can see it

catching the glare of the sun.

All that glass lit up.

You have to shield your eyes. Bright.

Quite a thing to see.

Quite a thing.

Latest Multi-Use Metaphor:
putting shellac on soap bubbles
Feel free to employ in any situation where the need arises. Recently had great success with it while attempting to illustrate cinema's relationship to fantasy.

When she spots you in her purr-if-real vision, you'll know right away if she likes what she sees.

"Our waiter: an assault of charming insincerity."

68

One more generation of millions engaged in a lifetime of desperate résumé writing will lead to the death of prose.

Haven't we all, at one time or another, countered the sensation of slipping into oblivion by grasping at some little genealogical factoid?

The Fez

I am resigned to wearing the fez
and standing at the hero's side--
a eunuch-y air and aura,
but dapper,
trim in my white suit, exotic
whiskers, loyal but
ultimately inscrutable.
I may have one or two
unspeakable appetites,
but the hero isn't invested
in such substitutions and differals.
I don't leave messes or corpses,
just empty bowls and ashes.
He pursues justice and fresh beds
while I click my tongue.
No passion is true
since the loss of the library
in Alexandria.
I sleep with ancient grudges.
I make a sullen companion,
but I'm useful for reading
old documents, decoding
lore, sharing my familiarity
with each local custom.
For a lifetime I resisted the role,
floating out of body in incense
and endless transmigration,
lost in my own faint haze.
Now I wear the fez
and no one asks questions.

A little time to kill in Barnes & Noble, so I sit down with Swann's Way...

This is the new translation by Lydia Davis. Says on the back cover she got a MacArthur Genius Grant. I had a French professor in college who told me French people don't read Proust. It's in what's called a literary tense, he said. Probably the equivalent of my trying to converse casually but couching everything in "at this point last year I would have been such and such..." I can imagine such an attempt to sustain verbally those kinds of constructions might lead me to stutter. I'm going to skip the introduction and go right to *Combray I*. Otherwise it's like holding back in some way. My reluctance to verbalize in social gatherings has often been characterized as "withholding." I like this chair. My daughter once described these chairs as squishy. But I think this one's pretty nice. *Metempsychosis*. Good word. A touch arcane. I wonder if Proust is using it wryly. I wonder if it was a literal translation. Probably have to be with a word like that. Can't imagine Lydia Davis thinking a genius grant is license enough to plug in a word like that on a whim. I wonder if this is the official Christian Reading Pit since it sits in the middle of the Christian shelves. If it is, I'm not sure I should be here with Swann's Way. I feel almost aggressively humanist. Pinter was profoundly affected by reading Proust; it changed his artistic agenda, some say. Many long and moment to moment descriptions about what it's like to wake up from a dream. The "artist as psychologist" is how the summaries like to summarize it. Heh, heh, summarize Proust. Wait a minute, the woman who just sat down on my right has a book with SEX on the cover. Either she, too, is being aggressively humanist, or it's a book about Christian SEX. I can't tell. The man and woman pictured on the cover are wearing sweaters and look healthy and happy. There are no italics in Proust. I must confess I'm intrigued by the fact that the woman with the SEX book did not choose a SEX book with an African-American couple on the cover. She appears to be African American, and I want to know if her book choice indicates her lack of strident allegiance to some cultural camp, because you know there must be a number of

70

SEX books available targeting African Americans explicitly. Or if she has chosen the book because it is a Christian SEX book–and perhaps that is in fact why she feels safe and enclosed and un-self-conscious about sitting down with such a book in this pit–if it is a Christian SEX book, would she have chosen it due to not seeing any Christian SEX books with African Americans pictured in sweaters on the cover? Never thought of myself as aggressively humanist, per se. I bet my particular curiosity about the African American woman places me among the great unwashed. If that is true, surely dipping into *Swann's Way* counts for something. Fewer commas, too, than I would have thought; Proust looks nice on the page. I've started re-reading this paragraph at least three times. Do you think anyone will see me sitting here with *Swann's Way* and find it funny? If I've started re-reading a paragraph three times, how many times have I read it? How do I count the attempts? That was not a riddle with an amusing solution. Or a math problem. I will confess the decision to sit down with *Swann's Way* was formulated in my mind in advance as a kind of "living joke." I went to the P's on the shelf with the plan already well-baked. Somewhere in my mind a notion took shape about documenting my attempts to undertake a series of "living jokes." And writing a book. And, heart swelling with secret pride, I then saw it on a bargain table at Barnes & Noble. Just like I want someone to see me sitting here and get the joke. And the person who did see me and did laugh quietly, possibly silently, perchance inwardly, would walk away transformed, briefly relieved from suffering. Or, to confess to my true craven selfishness, the person, a metaphysical being in disguise, would walk away having registered me in some transcendent Book of Days. When I finish my coffee I will stop reading and tell my daughter and her friends I'm ready to go.

Clinically speaking:
The Hysteric wants the hole package.
The Obsessive is moored in the hole, summing
parts.
The Pervert swears he saw the hole thing.
For the Psychotic it's no holes barred.

Go Humor: I'd challenge you to a game, but I
don't have the stones.

--Damn. Finish already.
--Already finished? Damn.

Good slip today: "...in the great scream of things..."

"Did that tickle your fancy bone?"

Life Sentence

Had you been following a path in life which could conceivably lead to your speaking the word "insufficiencies" in a sentence and, further, perhaps even modifying it with the word "certain" to produce the phrase "certain insufficiencies," your path having shaped you as the sort of person who might call upon the phrase as a natural and spontaneous locution, now, as you entangle and ponder and imagine in response to this sentence that you are presently reading, engaged in a kind of unavoidable speculative exercise in which the phrase "certain insufficiencies" issues forth hypothetically, unfolding in a moment chosen by your own whim and notion of timeless fancy, you are now no longer on that particular path, it being a permanently lost possibility no matter what direction your present speculations may take, nor can you ever be on that path again, and had you been following a path on which the phrase did not exist, in whole or in part, as an instance of truly outrageous diction, as a needling and peculiar and perhaps indulgent articulation, as an option afforded a speaker in need of drawing precise distinctions and of truly tapping the nail into place, now you, too, will never be on that path again. Ever. Ponder that.

New Performance Methods

I'm currently working on something and it has become quite absorbing. I know I'm going in a fruitful direction because I ache when I cannot steal any writing time on a given day.

I am using my understanding of some Lacanian psychoanalytic concepts to formulate some new performance strategies. I'm letting the work move out from a nod to psychophysical (and psychoacoustic) performance traditions since I consider myself a product of those traditions. But, like a good Lacanian, I'm trying to problematize the place of the body in these methods. Not with a desire to invalidate anything, of course; just find a place at the table. Or to use another image: to find a new off-shoot.

I am trying to get to the point where I turn some of Lacan's variables–**S1, S2, $, a**–into active playing principles. I'm also finding a way to situate the notions of *desire* and *drive* in a working process which will try to be both psychophysical and more rational at the same time. And most ambitiously, I'm taking Lacan's final ideas on the notion of the *symptom*–as both a kind of terminal effort at identification and as a working "know-how"–and trying to establish a group approach to a particular set of materials as a way of working in what I want to call a particular *symptomatic atmosphere*. And I'm attempting to render it all in an everyday language, not remotely like the shorthand jargon I've just employed. Some philosophical speculation, but I'm trying to keep it playful.

74

Thus far:

I warmly embrace the idea of improvisation being used as a method of research and plan to carry out some improvisational research in what follows. I ask you to be patient and stay with this one. It's going to take some time to prepare the field and start moving in the direction that interests me. My final aim is for some new structures to emerge that performers can use to explore and create. My process is improvisational and tentative. I will write as if I have you with me as a companion and sounding board, and I will assume you don't have a temperament for jargon or arcane concepts. I'm ultimately after something new to do and a way to explain it using everyday language.

The kind of performer I will be speaking to is one who is interested in the psychophysical and in what I am tempted to call the psychoacoustic (if you favor methods claiming Grotowski as a father, or "Eastern" body systems or martial arts as influential, or if you've worked with *Viewpoints* or the *Vocal Sequence*). In more commonplace actorly parlance, we are talking about processes which favor outside-in over inside-out strategies, methods in which emotional truths of a performance event emerge from the concrete actions and activities of the living body and not from more abstract processes of reflection, recollection, comparison, and identification. But since I plan in what follows to improvise with a psychoanalytically inflected discourse, already I'm not happy with what I've just said. From a psychoanalytic point of view, the easy distinctions I've just tried to employ comparing body-centered performance approaches to something else are less than helpful, leading me astray from my present interests and toward the usual deconstructables. Let's go with *performance methods*, instead. It's more neutral, more all-encompassing. I've grown reluctant lately to oppose outside-in to inside-out. I must admit that recently I've encountered some examples of psychophysical performance systems that have struck me dumbly in awe of their systematizing depth and integration of complex multi-cultural body calligraphies. But Actor's Studio strategies of recollection and em-bodied awareness are just other ways of asking for something unique from a physical system and are fair candidates to be included in the group of *performance methods*.

At any rate, it was in contemplating all of these diverse physical systems that I thought: the exoticism is the event. Any kind of system, whether body-centered or more "Method" in approach, has a certain self-sustaining, self-sufficient interest as a part of what it offers. It offers its performance events as novel and worth witnessing because of that novelty; its exoticism creates a ready-made stage frame. Any performance method has that built in. Watch, now, what the body undergoes as a result of this process. Certainly one could imagine psychophysical and Actor's Studio exoticisms fusing in a production of *A Streetcar Named Desire* "realized" by a cast of fifty Akido masters all of whom can cry on cue. We are not there to watch yet another performance of Williams' play. The play is incidental to the exotic bodily display. Watching Suzuki's *King Lear* I sensed that the true event was registered in my wonder at the perpetual crouch of the performers and the machine-gun intensity of their vocalizing.

What is exotic in a performance system (I am not yet sure why I am doggedly insistent on using this word exotic, I'm guided by an instinct that may or may not prove to be right) is expressed in what the system does with the performer's body. Every system has a definition of the body (explicit or implied) and an ideal vision of the body's possibilities, and, consequently, it asserts an aesthetics and an ethics as it operates on and with the body. What the body is and does is going to determine the nature and art of the performance. By all means, say it: Duh! And now I know why I wanted to begin this improvisational thinking-through by mentioning psychophysical performance methods.

In every performance system there is a knowledge of and for and in the body (most explicitly and comprehensively elaborated, perhaps, in psychophysical systems). By finally asserting this primacy of a body knowledge, I am able to focus my psychoanalytic view and ask: Is there a way to formulate a performance method (psychophysical, psychoacoustic, "Method," or otherwise) *that does not know what a body is?* Psychoanalysis, through the influence of Lacan, has become an inquiry not just into our past experiences and their residual traces on our psyches but also into types of knowledge and ways of knowing. "Knowing a truth" has been problematized as both a claim and an activity. Establishing a knowledge system is a process as beset with ambivalence and equivocation as is our navigation of personal desires and our management of symptomatic suffering. If I'm after a psychoanalytically engaged performance system–which I am: through this improvisation my purpose is becoming clearer--then by acknowledging an ignorance of the body, I'm making a good start. Lacan assures us that ignorance is an important part of a proper analytic stance. It follows, too, that if I do not know what a body is, then, by extension, I do not know a great deal, since we posit the body as either a source or a constituent component of many things. As we're dwelling in such spacious ignorance, other kinds of truth might emerge.

If we place the body under a question mark (I'm not advocating erasing all evidence of a body ever being present, mind you; that would hardly be possible, this is more about questioning knowledge rooted in the body and how we perform with such knowledge), a given of conventional wisdom suddenly becomes a problem. Consider:

Maybe, because of your fancy deconstructive sophistry, I can't tell you in so many words what a body is, but I still know it when I see it. And Dr. Johnson kicks the stone, "...thus."

Here, the knowledge of what a body is is grounded in the experience of seeing something. Prior to words, systems, and interpretations there is the facticity of what is there before you.

The fundamental confirmation. Akin to other fundamental recognitions and confirmations leaning on tautology: I am I, you are you, this is it, here we are. Meaning and understanding, and a basis for building knowledge, rest on an experience of recognition, on the presence of the image. To know our body because we link a set of sensations with a body we see, either someone's body out there or the whole of our own in a reflection, is a way of grounding an experience of truth, of meaning. But if we don't know what a body is, then we are placing this pre-discursive certainty in question. "We don't know it when we see it; we don't know what we are seeing."

So if we try to work with a performance system that does not know what a body is, you can begin to see we are moving toward something rather strange.

One quick thought experiment to help you see just how strange. Try to imagine a human being who is born into and raised within an environment in which all reflective surfaces have been removed (going outside is fine, but no ponds or standing water). Aside from that, a perfectly "normal" upbringing (seeing a reflection in the eyes of others would be the only glimpse which it would be impossible to eliminate unless the mother avoided eye contact…). How would this child learn? How would he or she come to have an identity? How would the person learn language? What all would be affected by removing the experience of "seeing yourself?" And what of the experiences of those blind from birth? Do they have experience of a fundamental semblance on which to build? Is the lack of image somehow compensated for in another way or does another structure develop? How does coming to understanding differ and how is it the same compared to those with sight? And how do we who see find a basis on which to understand how their experience might be different? How does lacking an image affect one's experience of sexual difference? (A Lacanian might speak of how the image does not ground meaning solely through what is seen, necessarily, but through a person's early attempt to organize a number of conflicting drives, with actual vision being only one small component; the blind have plenty of other drives they are attempting to organize into a meaningful "image." The idea of drives is going to be important in this psychoanalytic performance method, so I'll return to it soon.)

So now let's take stock of where we are with this new performance method we're trying to formulate. We are saying that we don't know what a body is: that right there is pretty strange and promising for our approach. Pretty exotic. Unique. I'd pay to see a performer who didn't know what a body was. I have no idea what that would look like or be like. The truth is, however, as I think about it, as if I am to be that performer who does not know what a body is, I have to wonder what I am supposed to do. If I don't know what a body is, what am I to be exotic with? I also have to admit that anytime the word body is used, I would be lying if I said I had no response, no experience of familiarity or understanding. We are all fairly sophisticated here, too savvy for me to get away with coyness. When I say that I do not know what a body is, we all know I am talking about new ways of organizing information, of finding new ways to uncover material for exploration. Other words can be used, of course. Other "bodily" issues can be examined and findings diverted into a new channel around more traditional ways of talking about them. Our methods are striving to express experience in new ways, all previous certainties in the concept of "body" always now followed by a question mark.

Perhaps this reliance on a phrase, *I don't know what a body is*, is trying your patience. Such a statement, you may think, is meaningless outside of a context or without reference to a set of particulars. Yes. And such questions of context and particulars are at the very heart, I think, of where our method is going.

78 Begging your patience, I want to stay with the body a moment longer. There's more I want to do, and it will, I hope, move us into a very particular and distinctive landscape. I'm going to take the word body and do some associating. These associations are mine alone, but my hope is that enough of what I uncover is material many of us share to acknowledge a principle or two. For me, body, as a unit of meaning or as that which can point toward meanings, interferes with its own reception. Here's a classic instance of Freudian overdetermination: the word body, no matter the context, no matter the speaker, presents itself to me co-mingled with a subtle atmosphere of sexual arousal. Linking it with a definite article does very little to temper the effect. It's an instance in which, no matter the context and no matter the particulars, body draws vectors from whatever arbitrary elements happen to be surrounding the word at any particular moment and directs them to a very specific place, nailing me to that place without fail. This dimension of the word body is there whether I want it to be there or not. Why is it there? I doubt my response is shared universally by English speaking people, but I am also sure I am not alone. Ask yourself what the word body triggers for you. If the word body can occupy a meaningful place in some kind of system of "objective" knowledge, it can also be a complicator of meaning, a disruptor of understanding. I don't know what a body is. The word body seems to know more about

me than I do about it, no matter the particulars or the context.

I have been dwelling on the idea of body, since, in psychophysical matters, the idea of the body plays an ambitious part in founding a knowledge and a method. In contrast with the idea of the body and how it lends itself to a particular concern, the word body is overladen with a network of conflicts and confusion. In psychoanalytic terms, this is how desire presents itself. Body is one thing as an element of discourse, as a factor in the expression of knowledge, and as the supposed object of examination, but it is quite another as what can be called a signifier of desire. What, then, in this psychoanalytic performance method, is the body to do? If there is no body knowledge and no coherent body spectacle, what constitutes the event? Where lies the investigation? What is explored? How do we realize this strangeness inherent in a performance which doesn't know what a body is?

Body is a word. *Body* is not *corpus*. *Corpus* is another word. Perhaps it would be clearer to say we want to perform without thought of a *corpus*, without knowing how to constitute a *corpus*. A *corpus* lies still, we assume, and can contain a multitude of potential notions. A *corpus* can be studied, systematized, manipulated. *Body*, as a word, has this extra quality; we note in our response to it that its function as a linchpin of understanding is almost superseded by its work as a signifier of desire (and yes, if I continue to associate, *corpus*, too, is clotted with extra substances, pointing as it inadvertently does to the sacramental and the necrophilic; clearly signifiers of desire lurk everywhere). If a word is functioning as a signifier of desire, then, what is it doing? Lacan's response, leaning upon Freud's research into how the unconscious works, would be: a signifier of desire is always pointing to other signifiers. Where, then, does the potential for movement lie in our performance method given we don't know what to say about the body? From signifier to signifier. Lacan uses some variables: from **S1** to **S2**.

What would it mean if a performer dispensed with everything but these variables? Obviously I'm leading up to the assertion that a great deal lies waiting for the performer in these variables and in their relation. Once we say we are going to occupy the world of meanings, let's even say that we might just consent to regard the world of meaning from a certain distance, then we are contending with **S1** and **S2**. As performers, let's avoid seeking definitions for a moment and just work with our instincts. I offered the observation that these two variables hold the potential for movement; I also suggested they are responsible for any experience of meaning. Movement as meaning? Am

I talking about literal physical movement? I am tempted not to try and answer that. As a performer perhaps it would serve you to not have that certainty. Look at the two variables: there is a sameness and a differentiation at work simultaneously. In what lies the sameness? In what the differentiation? I'm going to be a little cute here, I know: the variables share the letter while being distinguished by the number. Letters are the stuff of a language, the material available; numbers indicate the possibility for some kind of organization of that material, the relations and distinctions at work. Number also implies an infinite set of possibilities for organizing the stuff of the language. It's the number at work on the stuff which implies time and a relationship: not then, but now, not here, but there. We can deploy some other markings with our variables and kind of emphasize the notion of meaning in movement: $S1->S2$, and with that basic one established we can explore other possibilities, $S1<-S2$ or $S1<->S2$. To use just two variables and one or two arrows is to distill and abstract a great deal; it would be more accurate to render a very complex web of variables and arrows. But contemplating two variables can call forth a number of questions that might be passed over as we chart out a web of meanings. Is there anything before $S1$? Given the infinite nature of our network, is it truly possible to speak of an originary variable? What would it mean to regard an $S1$ as unique? And so on to the idea of the $S2$ if we grant $S1$ a special place. What are the implications? And if we see the possibility for the $S2$ to not only point forward to future S's but also back to the $S1$, what are the implications?

Linkages, chains, nets, networks, passages, synapses, circuits, connections. As a performer you could imagine sparking jumps from node to node, carrying the impulse of an arrow from an $S1$ to an $S2$. You can also imagine being the variable and offering yourself in a relation with another performer who holds the place of another variable, or you imagine that the arrow moves through the attentions of an audience. You can see the net as already existing and your play involving a tracing of the strands, or you are revealing links in the very act of seeking passage. Infinite free play, the workings of an associative machine. In a sense, you are attempting to realize the impossible free play of meanings in systems liberated from…what? In our state of imaginary freedom, we are not yet talking about desire. In many ways, to move with desire is to acknowledge you have certain limits on your movement, as if your feet are shackled. This is another way to talk about signifying chains. Desire is limitation to free play. Desire is what makes $S1$ and $S2$ particular for an individual, it's what makes the numbers count out a history. It's desire's grappling with particular limits that moves speech, and in the questing and questioning movement from signifier to signifier, the speaking subject is revealed. Where meaning is concerned, what is it that we rely upon? How is it that a jump from an **S1** to an **S2** can be experienced as meaning? And by what? The *subject*: that which can embody (the body appearing, again) a question, that which can experience meaning in the movement among signifiers. As a performer in this psychoanalytic system, you are a desiring subject, moving from signifier to signifier in a fashion weighted and inflected by desire. How is such movement accomplished? By any means ("necessary"). By speech. Through the unfolding of an event. Through "movement." By means of your "body." And always in a relation (**S1<−>S2**). Lacan offers a variable for the *subject* (you can use a question mark, certainly, but its physical appearance prevents access to certain qualities of the subject important in psychoanalysis): **$**.

Another variable. And there's at least one more on the way. And I'm reluctant to offer absolute, or "psychoanalytic," definitions for these variables because I want our performer's instincts to work with them as true variables, as place holders and possible positions, as points around which ideas might begin to gather. I want only to define these variables with respect to one another and maybe, later, to just a few other psychoanalytic concepts. How, then, can a performer make sense of this **$**, this subject? Let's start, as we did with our **S1** and **S2**, by noting the variable's graphic reality and, again, running the risk of being too cute (I'm imagining some teachers and colleagues rolling their eyes), seeing what that brings to mind. Another **S**, we note. In other words, in some ways we see more of the same. Yes, *signifier* and *subject* both start with **S**, which is accidental, yet it's also useful; this commonality of the **S** has been exploited to fullest in this system. Another signifier is at issue, as is the stuff of language. The *subject* is seeking a *signifier* which will fully meet its needs. The subject is trying to find itself in language. And to touch specifically upon the psychoanalytic origins of this, we might say it is trying to find itself in speech. The subject seeks a signifier for itself. But no signifier can stand alone and point only to the subject. The subject, in fact, knows this and wants the signifier to point past it in a way, to a beyond; the signifier, in fact, is always in part pointing to a beyond because it points to other signifiers. The subject is also referred to as the "subject of desire" since it is perpetually caught up in this quest among signifiers for identity and linkage and something beyond. Simple example: "How can I possibly put this into words?" Or: "The word escapes me." Or: "Do you understand?"

Or: "What am I saying?" Notice the $ has a line through it (the true Lacanian variable is divided by a diagonal slash, but I take what my HTML editor offers). The subject is a *divided* subject. What we want to say, no matter how articulate or gifted we are as pundits or raconteurs, does not perfectly coincide with the speech we, in truth, produce. Often we are painfully aware of this; often we are not until someone points it out to us. My favorite way of imagining this (which I confess just occurred to me, confirming for me again the value of an improvisatory approach) is to think of the slash as creating two mirrored and then reversed isomorphic halves of the S. The slash also produces a magnetic polar charge which interferes with the halves being able to join. As with two like-charged sides of magnets, the closer you try to bring the halves together, the more they slip and slide out of synch; never will they join and complete the S. This impossibility of union is also how we account for the interminable nature of desire. The slash is also meant to evoke the division between conscious and unconscious. And what is the division between conscious and unconscious if not a gap between those meanings to which we aspire and a certain fixed nature of our being over which we have no control? Often from a Lacanian you will hear some variation of the expression "the unconscious lies in the Other." This fixed nature of our being in a sense belongs to some Other because only this Other can see it and say something about it. Our subject, then, our $, is always caught between what it knows and wants and attempts to achieve through speech, and a certain crucial truth which will always be out of reach because it belongs only "to the Other." As a performer, are you not perpetually caught between your aim and intention to connect with an audience and that question of the audience's willingness to accept you and your presence? An audience's want is rooted in some aspect of your being over which, no matter your skill and conscious charm, you have no control. Or to put it in very universal human terms: "Why is it that I cannot make that which I love love me in return?" We want the Other to see us as lovable, but we cannot control, ultimately, what the Other sees. And we are hard pressed to accept any measure of truth in what the Other sees unless we have somehow managed to create and control it. The knowledge that lies in the Other: we don't want to know anything about it.

So with our three variables we can begin to find positions in structures. And depending on the positions, these variables can mean different things. These variables and positions can be offered up as a creative source of material. In the place of a *performing body* we offer *movement among variables*. It's easy to see how the subject ($) can be positioned between things, as either a stumbling block or a victim caught in the middle: **S1–>$–>S2**. Or we can see a subject attempting to complete a circuit in an effort to achieve some measure of self-understanding or successful communication: **$–>S1–>S2–>$**. Or we can use our slash to denote something out of the subject's reach, something in the domain of the Other: **$–>S1/S2**. Lacan proposed a theory of discourse which uses these variables in various positions to theorize various uses of speech; its tempting to see the resulting structures as so many little scenes. Just looking at the few structures I've offered as examples you can see how situations or struggles or events might emerge. Lacanian theory, however, has an extra variable. We have arrived at the phrase "last but not least."

Desire emerges, we have proposed, as a subject caught up in the limits of language trying to gain access to a certain sense of the beyond. The subject relies on signifiers to achieve its goal. Signifiers are words, symbols, signs, images, sounds, anything through which we try and transmit to others that which we have to transmit, anything which allows the subject to move what it feels inside to an outside and to the Other and then back. The Other essentially says, "Here, you can use these things to attempt to make contact." Psychoanalysis proposes that this signification process is imperfect. There are things inside which cannot be translated through a signification process. There are things which stay unsymbolizable. And that means, in a way, there are things beyond the grasp of the subject. Not only is there something that cannot be symbolized, but since it cannot be symbolized it will not be altered or modified in the translation process. The subject is aware of its existence but is not in a position to work on it through signification. Now, am I indulging in a kind of mythologizing or just reflecting on some aspect of common experience? I am, I think, offering one inflection of something common to human experience which can also be described by the word "unspeakable."

The unspeakable. There's an essay topic for you. Yes, take it in all of its meanings, connotative and denotative. Imagine a white room in an art gallery. The artist's installation consists of a number of white cards placed on the walls each with a different word printed upon it in black ink. The words: I would rather not reproduce them here because they are all unspeakable. Nothing in the room but these white cards with words, but you, the observer, might begin to feel the presence of something else, something palpable and palpitating and perhaps unpleasant or perhaps arousing. The truth of your response is beyond your ability to speak it away or rationalize it.

The soprano's nose starts to bleed as she sings the National Anthem. There is a truth present beyond what we want (and one, perhaps, we all try not to talk about). And yet…it is also possible to be fascinated.

Or to temper this beyond and offer it in a different way: "One day I'll find a way to show people what I truly am like…" We express that wish but then we might find ourselves renouncing such a thought as we are unable to locate the division between that inner sense of warm abundance we wish to share and the questionable scenario playing out on some shadowy private stage. Both the inner warmth and the shadowy drama seem to partake of a common substance. A substance, I might add, which vaporizes the minute you make an attempt to signify it.

Where is this beyond located exactly? Is it hidden away in us or does it lay waiting for us in the Other? Why can't we put it into words or at least determine if it's inside us or out there? Do we want to, really? This situation is represented by our fourth variable: **a**. In French, *Autre* is the word for Other; we could see the little **a** as meaning *a little piece of the Other*. So the **a** is a thing, a something, an object, an unspeakable thing, something so intimate we're not even sure if it's actually a part of us or part of something else, something missing and residing elsewhere. Is the beyond within or without?

Remembering our desire to find a way to perform without knowing what a body is, I want to say that through the **a**, the body returns to us in a strange and unrecognizable way. Yes, in an unspeakable way.

But that doesn't stop us from trying to speak it. Or make it speak to us. Trying to make the body signify something with our assorted psycho-physical systems, our performance strategies. All the ways we attempt to tap in to this body as a meaning source, from activated sense memories to chattering chakras to leaping tigers. This **a** compels us to grasp for something essential; its unspeakable nature captivates us. In fact, this subject of ours ($) is forever attempting to come to grips with it. We can even write a structure for the effort: $<>**a**. The subject attempts the impossible. How? By putting it into words (S1->S2)? And not getting it quite right. Words fail. What, then, is prior to the words, or what can bring the subject closer and bypass the words? Will images do it? Will some kind of overladen distortion of words do it? Again, I am making reference to that shadowy scene playing out on a shadowy stage. In psychoanalytic parlance, this **$<>a** is called the structure of fantasy. Let's see it lurking beneath every effort at signification:

S1->S2/$<>a. Let's see it also as fixed in the midst of the signifying chain: **S1->($<>a)->S2**. Could we call this *what is imagined rupturing what can be spoken*? Or, alternatively, *what is imagined inflaming what can be spoken*? I want to assert that much of a performer's effort dwells at this level, through working with this structure. Until I get to a point where I can offer my ideas about how, practically, this might happen, see what you make of it. Try some experiments with our four "placeholders": **$, S1, S2, a**. You might use them to analyze some common situation we share. What in such a situation can we associate with each variable and how, then, do they interrelate? Or try dressing each variable with some particular "colors" and associating each with some particular actions. Use the variables to chart a certain bodily ordeal. Now, about the *drives*...

To begin to understand the *drives*, I should say, first, that I did clean the **a** up a bit for its first appearance and introduction. So far my descriptions have touched on the mystical, the metaphysical, hinting, perhaps, that the **a** is a *via negativa* leading on a good day to a divine communion. I'll set that possibility aside and say that where the drives are concerned, the **a** is a target for a powerful longing, a longing so primal and constitutional to us as living beings, it is best to think of it as existing prior to all notions of experience and identity. The site of this longing is the body (whatever that means...perhaps we are talking about the biological organism at this point...perhaps) in relation to some Other presence, a presence which seems to be a source for sensation and sustenance. The Other establishes a link between meanings and stimulations for the body, a kind of very primitive vocabulary the body is driven to use to pursue this Other connection, this Other's perpetually extended offer of completion. This bodily longing for completion is intimate; everywhere it is possible for the body to open itself to the world (and therefore to the Other) the drive for the **a** exists. And at each of these openings there is the possibility of an object the Other might share. If you are familiar with Freud you may have encountered mention of these drives, the oral and anal being two examples, with food (the mother's breast) and feces being those drives' complementary objects. Lacan goes so far as saying that everywhere on the body where there exists a rim (mouth, anus, urethra, ear, eyelid), there exists a drive toward an **a** and an object for that drive (food, feces, urine, the phoneme, the gaze) trying to serve as the **a**. These drives are called partial drives because they are not constituent pieces of some whole or parts of some master co-

85

ordinated system. Partial and disorderly they remain, driving without cessation or compromise toward the promise of the **a**. In Lacanian terms, then, to be subject (**$**) to a fantasy (**$ <> a**) is to believe it is possible to come to some arrangement with the drives, to find an image which will coordinate the drives and answer them totally. If we use the word "grip" to represent the unpredictable nature of our linking term (<>), then we can say in fantasy we are always either trying to "get a grip on" or we are "in the grip of" our drives.

Let us dispense with the body, then, and the promise of coordinated completion such a notion implies, and speak of drives. In fantasy, perhaps, we try to resolve things through an image of the body. In day to day activity, in our active implementations of intentions, in our struggle to make moments of life cohere as meaningful paragraphs, we might say, "This is my body. This is what my body does." As performers we might use such thought in our preparations and explorations, and it might efficiently serve us. But if we explore possibilities for a "body" in a psychoanalytic framework, we try to see the uncoordinated work of drives beneath the agency of the body. In fact, we can see the "body" as a signifier, an **S1**, and we can see the installation of an **S1** as a sublimation of the work of the drives. For a moment we can position the **a** at just the right distance from such a signifier, we can have fantasy shimmer in just such a way beneath the signifier, and we can control the dispersion of meaning as the **S1** yields to inevitable movement toward **S2**, and we can isolate the **S1** as an instance of something rare and particular, as the ideal. Within the Other, this **S1** occupies the honored spot; it's a signifier shining forth as the embodiment of an essence. Our poor subject (**$**), looking toward the Other for guidance, is offered the **S1** as the place where everything starts (and ends). And how tempting it can be as a performer to believe that within the Other there is a place where everything starts and ends, particularly if you can position yourself to seem to stand within such a place and as a part of such a signification–and to act with a conviction because your method, your know-how (**S2**), is tailor made to serve the ideal (**S1**).

In our psychoanalytic performance method, we resist saying things start and end with the **S1**. We choose ignorance over mastery, questions over assertions, trivial details over true guidelines, inchoate drives over blueprints. And, yes, it's fun to find myself suddenly marching to the rhythms of a manifesto. I hadn't planned on things moving in that direction. It's insidious the way the **S1** sneaks up on you. Let me try and get a grip by assuring you that I am making my strong assertions in an effort to formulate something about a practical working method, and this will be my last bit of theoretical speculation. Ignorance over mastery, questions over assertions, trivial details over true guidelines, messy drives over clean blueprints: I would like to conjure up something I will call a *symptomatic atmosphere* and ask for it as the minimal set of conditions necessary for psychoanalytic performance work.

This is difficult. I have known for some time that I wanted to develop this idea of a symptomatic atmosphere as a fundamental condition for psychoanalytic performance, but now that the moment has arrived, I find myself stalling out a bit. It's perhaps because the concept of the symptom, thanks to Lacan, has gotten pretty complicated and contentious, and I make no claims for having sorted it all out. How to begin? Talk of the symptom is often connected with what Lacan asserts are the three orders of experience, so maybe I will get somewhere by giving my nod to those.

Somewhere along the way, Lacan decided that the ultimate visual aide for furthering psychoanalytic education and theoretical elaboration was the knot. Why? This may come across as a bit flip, especially since I am not a mathematician and can't really back up what I'm about to say, but I think the knot is an ultimate way for topology to materialize *impossibility*, and it was always the materialization of impossibility, the attempt to bring paradox to flesh, that Lacan found most intriguing about topology. Do you actually have to know anything about the mathematics of topology to appreciate the use of knots in psychoanalysis? I think an appreciation for the *mystique* is quite sufficient, and, after all, psychoanalysis appeals, I think, to those of us who desire to acknowledge a nebulous thing like mystique as a powerful and concrete functional principle. Additionally, knots allow for linkages of heterogeneous elements, hence their usefulness in characterizing the three linking orders: *the Symbolic, the Imaginary,* and *the Real.*

Let's imagine a knot made up of three distinct rings which interlink in such a way that each link appears to guarantee the cohesion of the structure. In other words, if you cut any one of the three links, the knot falls apart, the links are set free to float off on their own. This knot (called a *Borromean,* by the way) is one way to look at human reality as the interlinking of three rings, realms, domains, concepts, what have you. Their interlinking and interdependence is our reality. One link can be called the Imaginary. It's the way we organize reality based on what's there in front of us, on the image, on what we see. As living creatures, we react and respond to what we see. We make judgements and determinations. We formulate meanings: "Oh, I *see*...I get it." And self-understanding: "We have much in common. We are so *similar*." And ascertain threats: "You are not to be trusted." Imaginary dynamics work through a binary process consisting of you and some other and a resolution through a perception. The image, the essence of a sense of either/or, is very basic, primitive, and powerful. Images cohere and guide our feelings. And things are, indeed, what they seem to be and are, indeed, shaping the core of our emotions in this realm of the Imaginary. (As an aside, I often wonder: if our dominant sense were smell instead of sight, as it is with dogs, would we have to call it the Olfactory rather than the Imaginary? But it would organize our reality in the same way: sight or smell is telling us whether something is good or bad, dangerous or beneficial, friend or foe, etc.)

The second link, the Symbolic, can be most perversely illustrated through William Burroughs' observation that *language is a virus*. We are organisms that have to a certain extent become hosts to a vital system whose survival and mechanisms are beyond our control. We are "subject" to the laws of language, we are subject to the laws of the land, we are subject to the laws of technology and physics. For every **S1** there is going to be an **S2**, such is the law, and we can believe that we are responsible for all of the linkages, but most take place whether we take a hand in them or not. Ancestry and the workings of kinship are vivid examples of the Symbolic order. Whether we want to acknowledge the fact or not, all of us are sons and daughters, all of us have names floating in our wakes we did not choose. Or consider the old verity: "Ignorance of the Law is no excuse." The farthest-reaching implication of that statement is that there are, written on assorted pieces of paper somewhere (or floating in cyber-space,) a series of marks which, unbeknownst to you, will perhaps determine one day how you will spend the rest of your life and how you will die. I do not mean to dwell upon the notion of helplessness as I try to illustrate the Symbolic. Obviously it is possible to act as a capable player in the Symbolic universe (using the Imaginary to conjure us into the image of capability and self-confidence, of course). But from the point of view of psychoanalysis, the workings of the unconscious rely on symbolic mechanisms (it's the only way to produce any sort of content, after all), so it's crucial to understand the ways in which the **S1->S2** functions under the radar and out of sight.

One link we can call the Imaginary; another, the Symbolic. Our third link, with the peculiar name of the Real, might be described (given the way in which the Symbolic and Imaginary seem between them to have reality covered) as anything that doesn't work. This definition of the Real is close to a way to talk about symptoms, but more of that later. The Real is what cannot be articulated or explained. The Real is what neither notions of identity nor an encyclopedia can address. And, yes, the Real is a certain kind of living experience that leaks beyond the edges of the Symbolic and the Imaginary. It gets its own link in the knot because it can have its own kind of precision, incision, and repetition--something inscribed in flesh but not fleshed out. Remember that our three links are heterogeneous, yet interlinked; the Real, however, is harder to speak about as a separate theoretical component. The notion of the Real has its origin in psychiatric and psychoanalytic experience and can best be thought of in connection with the horrors and bafflements of psychosis. For us as performers, it's perhaps most useful to think of the Real as a sense of outer limit or a dead end or some unbidden bodily expression or experience. Often anxiety is spoken of as an indicator of something in the Real being at issue.

To speak of a particular human being, then, is to speak of the interlinking of these three rings into a knot. For a psychoanalytic performer, the links and ways they knot define a terrain for investigation. Our variables—$, S1, S2, a—offer paths and positions within that terrain. Desire and drive perhaps describe modes of travel or the types of maps available. A symptom describes the climate. Clearly I want it to elaborate upon the climate since I want to give life to this notion of symptomatic atmosphere. Let's see the symptom in psychoanalytic experience as a progression, as a movement through various ways of experiencing x, where **x** designates what it always tries to designate: the unknown. (Using this definition, our initial curiosity about "what is a body" could be seen as a symptomatic expression: "Doctor, I woke up this morning and suddenly realized I don't know what a body is." This is good. We want to create a symptomatic atmosphere with such notions.)

Our unknown x, then, is a question, and therefore a part of the speaking subject, $. In a classic psychoanalytic structure consisting of an analysand and an analyst, our unknown **x** begins its progression as a question or concern or complaint or demand the analysand poses to the analyst about something that no longer seems to work the way it should. That is the nature of a symptom at the outset. Through the symptom some bit of the Real, one of our three links in reality, appears in a new and unsettling way. Why does the analysand pose the question to the analyst? Because the analyst (often in the guise of doctor or therapist or teacher or confidant) is supposed to know something about it, to have some privileged knowledge of the Real, and may even have an answer. If things move forward as they do in psychoanalysis, the unknown **x** is not met with an answer or prescription. The analyst, rather, directs our questioning subject back to this mysterious **x** and encourages him or her to find the x's place within the knot that makes up the analysand's (the patient's) individual reality, that particular knotting of the Real with the Symbolic and the Imaginary. The existence of the x, this new manifestation of the Real, is tied in there with everything else.

As this knot is worked over (it's not exactly something you could un-tie, nor would you want to) in the presence of the analyst, the nature of the unknown **x** progresses through an interesting transformation. The analyst is no longer seen as a Master of the Real (or of the Symbolic or Imaginary for that matter) and instead takes up a more intimate and troubling position as the cause of speech itself, perhaps the cause of desire itself. The analyst becomes part of the nature of the unknown x. At this point the **x** is considered a proper psychoanalytic symptom. This transformation of the **x** is actually seen as narrowing in to something more precise and particular for the subject. After that, things can get even more narrow and specific. You can perhaps begin to see how the questioning of the **x** can become the questioning of the a, that mysterious bit of the Other the subject isn't sure whether to seek within or without. The **x** takes on features of the a and so becomes caught up with consideration of the drives. To see the **x** in the Real of the drives is another extreme transformation.

What's next for the symptom, for the **x**? To borrow from Lewis Carroll, you talk until you get to the end and then you stop. And, according to Lacan, you stop because the subject is finally able to see the **x** transform into some irreducible element, some "bit of nonsense," free of possible further questioning. Then the subject, in a touching coda, claims this final version of the symptom in an act of identification.

Such is the journey of the symptom. In light of that, what might it mean for a performer to work in a symptomatic atmosphere? At any given moment in this psychoanalytic method of ours, we can pursue, embody or resist meanings, and we can do so as we encounter three different presentations of the Other: in the Audience, in our fellow performers, and in our own physical reality. Isn't a symptom that which is, ultimately, at stake in any consideration of the Other? A symptom is a quest for the meaning of matter, a quest at all moments haunted by the possible non-meaning of matter. And, perhaps, that is the best statement of the climate of psychoanalytic performance work I can muster at present.

Ah, but what does it all look like? Demonstrations are in order, are they not? That's part of the excitement of any performance system, after all. They're so very demonstrable. And that is because, in part, the body knows its place. In my earlier questioning of the role of the body in a psychoanalytic method, I somewhat destabilized the place of the body. I have, in fact, through my thought and questioning, tried to trouble the body's Imaginary consistency. The idea of a performer's body only has consistency in the realm of the Imaginary; in the Symbolic and the Real there is no stabilizing image on which to rely. Stating this has just now allowed me to articulate a principle strategy for psychoanalytic performance: the psychoanalytic performer attempts to de-stabilize the Imaginary and then privilege activity in the Symbolic and the Real (same as in traditional psychoanalysis, actually). All of the concepts I've introduced so far from the four variables to the notions of desire and drive and symptomatic atmosphere can be used to both destabilize images of consensus and bring forward Symbolic and Real possibilities for exploration. To try and show this is, of course, is to step back into an Imaginary structure and offer the accompanying guarantees. But an example of some kind is in order. After all, even though I'm trying to dispense with a few reliable certainties, I am trying to offer performers some new things to do.

This idea of de-stabilizing the Imaginary will get unpacked more thoroughly as I go. For me this is one of the most interesting aspects of this performance approach because usually a performer is attempting to achieve a certain level of mastery and accomplishment within the Imaginary. A performance usually wants the Imaginary to ascend or at least achieve a certain undisputed prominence. Often a performer's goal is to help build a fantasy and then hold it in place while it works its magic. Get the audience to sign on the dotted line…

As I formulate the idea of de-stabilizing the Imaginary in order to bring forward possibilities within the Symbolic and the Real, I can't help but entertain thoughts of another possible strategy for a psychoanalytic performance approach. If there is a knot present, there is an attempt to loosen it, to understand it, to chart its workings and maybe reconfigure it. If a knot is distinctly not present, however, can one be tied? It's tempting to offer possibilities for two performance approaches, one for loosening knots and one for, dare we say it, tying them. We can propose two approaches as long as we understand that they may not be structurally complementary like, say, differential and integrative calculus (a mathematical analogy is always appealing because of the mathematical mystique). In the Lacanian view, if any of our three links are apart, you can't just link them and tape up the severed ends. Any attempt to link the rings is going to involve a compromise arrangement, perhaps one in which a link is doubled over in order to bind with the others or in which a fourth link is introduced as a way to bind the other three. In other words, a binding strategy has to be created. And if a fourth link is created to facilitate things, Lacan proposed in his later thought that this fourth link must be something of a symptomatic creation, a willed embodiment of meaning, and might this be an exciting possibility for us as psychoanalytic performers who attempt such a creation within our symptomatic atmosphere?

Yes, it can only get more obtuse and abstract as we start speculating about a fourth symptomatic knotting link.[1] Better to move on to something more tangible. Let's say we have enough theory for now.

---

1 This is the *sinthome* alluded to at the close of the Introduction to this collection.

Pirate's cheese of choice? "HAR-VAR-TEEEEE!"

Trotting dogs on the roadside out for a jolly scrounge. Ah, that's the life!

H line from abandoned abededary: Honea habitually hatcheting hyperbolic here-we-gos...

All the old pleasant trees...have been cut down.

The hairline in my profile photo has receded. Weird.

"On or around." Like that phrase. "On or around." 93

The way of the Whitmanesque loaf is lost in the smoke of the Information Revolution.

Cool and collected. UV protected.

Must smile and ignore more and more.

Snatches of a waking dream

We begin to establish our symptomatic atmosphere by agreeing we will not direct our bodies to do specific things in order to pursue some kind of "group training" through various body and behavior technologies. Along the same lines, we refrain from undertaking, as a group, any guided imagery. At the same time it should be said that body, behavior and imagination can be employed at any time, singly or collectively, to pursue questions of meaning or non-meaning. No instruction or training, just freedom.

Let me add at this point that any directions from a master should be subjected to some unknotting. Such directions usually fall under the heading of **S1** if issued by mandate or some version of an embodied voice, **S2** if a collection of guidelines or instructions that may at one time have been in a textbook. All **S2**'s have some **S1** lurking behind them somewhere. We can start to investigate our craving for such guidance through **$** and **a**. Or you can dislodge an **S1** by turning to other **S2**'s.

How and what do we perform? And who do we want to answer that question for us? Let me, rather, offer a thought that came into my head one evening as I was picking up my kids from the dance studio. I sat in the car and didn't go in right away. The clock stated I was ten minutes early. If I went in right away there was a chance I would have to make conversation with other waiting parents. I thought something like: *that would take too much out of me.*

That would take too much out of me. That thought may be all I want to offer at this point. You can try to ask me questions, but I don't have to answer them. What else was going through my mind as I drove to the studio? Did I have anyone specific in mind who I wished to avoid? What did I see that sparked my reluctance? Do I commonly avoid such situations? Something specifically about the dance studio, perhaps?

Am I willing to give more information? Perhaps doing so would take too much out of me.

So, as a performer, I've attempted to start evoking a *symptomatic atmosphere*. At this point I might want to make a decision. Do I want to speak? Maybe I offered my fragment (my specimen?), my *that would take too much out of me*, through speech, not as a bit of writing. Perhaps a fellow performer underlined the phrase as I was sharing material with the group my speech, speech now fragmented and examined by someone else. I need to think about whether or not I want to continue speaking or withdraw and let the fragment orient the work. If I continue to speak, there is the possibility that my fellow performers will want to explore the event of my speaking as they try to grapple with the content of my speech. They can choose to see me standing in the place of the subject ($). If I consent to stand in the place of the subject, I am offering my particularity to the group (my "story," my "body," my $S1$'s, $S2$'s, my **a**, my *desires* and *drives*). Of course, it is not an all or nothing situation for one participant. Any performer at any moment can choose to stand in the place of the subject, either by speaking or through some other signifying activity. What is useful, and really quite necessary, is for the performer to find a way to notify others the he or she is choosing to stand for the subject because there also needs to be "working communication" among performers that is free from suspicion and scrutiny (but not doubt and uncertainty, such things flowing back into the symptomatic atmosphere). The group, before working, can establish some kind of protocol for how speech will be used.

For the purposes of illustrating performance strategies and situating the role of a performing body that does not know what it is in such strategies, I'm going to try and simplify things by shutting my mouth at this point. *That would take too much out of me* is the last thing I'm going to offer as a subject (as a "speaking" subject

95

and obviously at present I'm not speaking but writing...

just try to go with it...). That little culminating phrase and the scrap of anecdote that led up to it are now there for the performers to explore. First, a warning about what to avoid.

Performers trained solely in traditional improvisational approaches will want to stay in the Imaginary register. Please don't stay in the Imaginary register. A traditional performance approach might involve an attempt to represent a situation that somehow illustrates the bit of anecdote or its culminating fragment, the performers striving to elicit sighs of recognition from the viewer. I'm even hard pressed to waste valuable typing time trying to write out an example of such a thing. A performer's hidden motive in such work is often re-assurance: re-assuring the audience through a display of the consensual and familiar and re-assuring him or herself that he or she's still "got it" (talent to entertain) and can still "get it" (some kind of approbation) from an appreciative audience. A psychoanalytic performer can always pass through the Imaginary register and bestow meanings on actions or create identifiable characters with familiar motives, but he or she is aware that imaginary elements are tools to employ and not the sole ends to attain. In the clinical realm, remember, to be "in the grip of the Imaginary" is to be convinced that the sad melodrama playing out in your mind's eye is true. This is not the truth our performers are after.

That would take too much out of me can be read in its entirety as either an **S1** or an **S2**. It can be a consequence or it can have consequences. As an **S2** it might be a cover-up for something, a way to distract or to stop discussion. What is a subject (\$) trying to do with such a phrase? How might the words be **S2** for some other **S1**? The word *that* is an **S2** for what **S1**? Or does it point toward an imagined act? A dreaded act?

Too much? If it's an **S2**, we can ask "too much of what?"

S2's can be pursued which elaborate upon *out of me*. Points to thoughts of me as some kind of container, perhaps.

Would has a certainty to it. A prediction. **S1** as an oracular pronouncement. As opposed to using *could*, a word urging caution. Something slightly presumptuous and grandiose about would. But it's also a question. To whom? Some kind of solicitation.

96 You could play with *take too much* as some kind of primal command (again **S1**).

Our fragment is wonderfully image-free. This moves us toward defining a relation to the **a**, toward a state of affairs that cannot be represented. **S1–>S2** can only rub up against it.

For \$<>**a**, explore the relational positioning implied and see all terms as reversible: *I would take too much out of you, I would take too little out of you, I am too much to take, I am too little to take, I want to be excessive, to be excessive you need me, you put too much into me, you can put too much into me, you can take too much out of me,* etc…

In terms of desire, something with the Other involving excess or parsimony.

In terms of drive, the quantification of a substance that can be held onto or lost is clearly anal in character, but you need not limit examination to the anal. Excess and parsimony with respect to mouth, voice, the visual, the rim as entrance and exit, the body/self as container, etc.

Let me back up a moment and touch upon something obvious. *That would take too much out of me* is a phrase that refers to a possibility of exhaustion. I don't mean to neglect that aspect of the phrase as I subject it to more interpretive manipulations. Certainly a performer can examine the whys and wherefores of a situation one wishes to avoid because it would be exhausting. And it is certainly not too obvious to explore the nature of the situation and the fear of exhaustion. The phrase is functioning as a metaphor in this instance. Even here **S1** and **S2** are at play. Why this particular substitution and not another? Why not employ the phrase *that would be too tiring*? In uttering the phrase *that would take too much out of me*, what desire might the subject be expressing? Why such a response in such a situation? Is there some compelling **S1** pointing to the more mundane notion of exhaustion which in turn is signaling to an **S2** like *that would take too much out of me*, some unspoken **S1** that quietly supports the subject's certainty or conviction. It is possible that the utterance is an instance of negation, of course, masking a wish for the very thing feared. **S1** and **S2** engaged in mutual deception.

S2 can often be used to point to wider realms of information and knowledge (as well as to that storehouse of "Other" knowledge working in the unconscious). Our phrase is an expression of economics. What linkages might be followed along those lines? How might *scarcity* point towards *death*?

How to do more with the **a**? It is with the **a** that a psychoanalytic performer can bring to bear the idea of embodied uncertainty, most immediately by following actions which heighten such uncertainty, by using their capacities to inscribe or write what I want to call events of *sensation, but not sense*. Lessons are available elsewhere on this site for using the Vocal Sequence, a useful method for finding ways to perform or inscribe such inscrutable moments. Other psychophysical methods can be employed. Inclusions of various media are possible. Think of it this way: Imagine the audience or a fellow performer occupying the place of the Other. You attempt to do something which can function as the most crucial and intimate aspect of the Other's being, as if you are attempting to restore the most important missing element, some piece that may even be beyond the scope of meaning. The psychoanalytic truth of this missing thing, however, is that we don't know whether it, this most intimate element, brings fulfillment or destruction or one enclosed within the other. Lacan called this most intimate twofold state of completion (an impossible state spoken of mostly as a substance) *jouissance*.

I had originally thought that I would succeed in putting together this speculation about psychoanalytic performance without mentioning *jouissance*. But I realized that if I want the psychoanalytic performer to employ methods structured by not knowing what a body is, I have to give some idea about what remains once the body of meaning is set aside. What's left is a body that is not yours. Maybe we can call it the Other's body. You can also call it the inscrutable body or the body of *jouissance*. Since we set aside all understanding of it, we are at the mercy of it as something Real, something un-mediated through meanings, something beyond desire, something moving through the drives to something else. End of the line, final stop: *jouissance*. It's meant to be the one true guiding star and very disorienting at the same time.

And overwhelming. How can a performer use such an idea to orient his or her efforts? There is no real way, after all, to talk about working with your *jouissance*. The poor subject would try to utter such a thing, perhaps, but in *jouissance* the subject vanishes. The psychoanalytic performer can work with a question, however, pertaining to *jouissance* as long as we think of it as the Other's *jouissance*. It's the Other's body (as *jouissance*) we are working with, after all. And it's there in thinking about the **a** and in the subject's vexing relationship with the **a**. Or is it possible to write a new **S1** guided only by the promptings from the body of *jouissance*. What kind of signifying architecture (through **S2**) can rest upon it?

98 Psychoanalysis itself can be summed up, I think, as an extremely long conversation about the Other's *jouissance* (with unavoidable transformative consequences, naturally). I'll be eager to hear if teachers and colleagues let that one stand (since I do realize I may be a bit reckless from a clinical point of view with such a characterization; such a preoccupation with the Other's *jouissance* is in many instances a feature of a psychotic structure; I'm thinking of ways in which a subject's fundamental questioning of the nature of the Other's *jouissance* can lead to certain neurotic solutions; obviously, the notion that the psychotic terrain can be explored creatively by a performer must be approached with great caution). Anyway, the psychoanalytic performer has as an option to orient actions toward the question of the Other's *jouissance*. (Surely our love of gossip and tabloids are two examples of our preoccupation with the Other's *jouissance*. This does not have to be an obscure concept.)

Back to our phrase. *That would take too much out of me.* Let it echo in the vertigo of your body's absence. Use the questioning of the Other's *jouissance* to compel your actions. Think of every arrangement of our four variables as an effort to do something about *jouissance*, to manage it, dissolve it, hide it, answer it, to (heaven forbid) obtain it. Your body, now accustomed to the uncertainties of being a body of *jouissance* rather than a body of meaning, enters the action in new ways, finds unexpected passages through the maze the variables set.

I think I've gotten about as inscrutable as I can get, so at this point I'll stop. If you as a performer find some new approaches or strategies using this "psychoanalytic orientation" and if it leads to new kinds of material and events, if it helps find new ways to employ the psychophysical, then it's been worth it.

I've kept my discussion as content-less as I possibly can.

Design Ideas

This happens every so often. I am captivated by a design concept and I have to note it ASAP. This is just a verbal description, right now. I'll try to get some visual work onto *vyew* eventually

What if any architectural elements of the Inn had a Georgian, Neo-Classical flavor? Part of Blake's charm and power as an artist came from his use of academic, classical conventions (well near Greek) in the service of his own unique visionary conceptions. Something almost temple-like about the Inn.

A Palladian dome as a central feature of the interior. The dome could tilt to various angles and take projections of everything from architectural design details to constelled stars to angels swirling about to acrobats tossing the sun and moon. This dome could also descend and rest on the stage as a pleasant green English hill.

The interior of the Inn would be perpetually "under construction" and we would see scaffolding stacked in the space, Blake standing upon it and working on various relief friezes, or one vast one, carving the images of the beasts he's tamed. The faces of tyger, rabbit, cat, cow, sun, moon, etc, could be removed from the reliefs as white masks. Children run with these white masks into the fireplace and reenter with the masks vividly colored and perhaps attached to billowing cloth, now ready to be treated as animated creatures.

Such a concept could be abstracted to a flat, two dimensional approach if we chose with the dome becoming a disk, the reliefs becoming sectional screen panels, etc.

But I keep coming back to this notion of Blake as a labouring presence, a creative presence…

Opening image inspired by this approach. Chorus stands in a shadowy, semi-circle. In their midst are two angels rotating a giant drafting compass upon the floor. We hear the chiming. As the circle is inscribed the Inn's floating dome begins to appear above: "this Inn belongs to William Blake…" "Many are the beasts he's tamed…" We discern Blake working upon a relief and we see the carved images about the temple-Inn.

I think we could have fun juxtaposing a kind of mystic, austerity with a more cozy, domestic, eccentric atmosphere created among the various inhabitants.

I'm thinking a blog title... ACTION AT A DIS-TANCE: aches & pains in the interstices of art, science, thought and politics.

Why do the monkeys fling their poo? They've been convinced it's really fertilizer feeding the growth of Liberty.

Beyond your reach then. Beyond your reach now.

101

Invited to meet up with old school chums. What's the best way to practice reminiscing?

Working Title: Comfort Foods of the Post-Human

Love. Lies. Bleeding.

Bookstore

I handed the girl my books and my discount card. She looked the titles over as she rang them up--a bit too much attention for my taste. Then, yes, a remark; I was tuned to its inevitability and tightened up a bit. I don't remember it exactly: "I love this one. Jane Eee-ree. Have you read it?" My discomfort was then instantly doubled, and I choked out something like: "It's on my daughter's summer reading list." She made another comment as she handed me my receipt, but I had withdrawn my attention at that point, and her curious speech patterns had garbled it anyway. I was dizzy with awkwardness. Was it a response? Something new? Taking it further? I smiled and offered a placating nod as I headed for the door.

O the thoughts I had. O the comments I formulated. O the irony I mustered. And of course it was a chain store, a floating ship of corporate mega-death. And so on.

It's been three days and I can't forget her smile. It was ceaseless, endless. It was present, fixed, from the moment I saw her see me approach the counter. It was, to use the formerly fashionable post-structuralist phrasing, "always already there." And it was obscenely authentic. Not polite. Not professional. Joyous. She seemed happy to be there doing what she was doing. Happy helping me. Happy to talk with a stranger about books.

102

She loved Jane Eee-ree. I have no way of knowing what reading is for her. Because, for one thing, I didn't ask her, even though I had the opportunity. She spoke of love. I offered distracting excuses for being there. Something about her radiated a truth about bookstores and why people read and why reading is a way to love. I'm the one who wanted the corporate exchange: just give me my empty abstract product and leave me alone.

I told myself she was in some way a "special needs" person, as if I needed to give myself a satisfying and condescending explanation of why I was so uncomfortable. But, really, after three days to think about it, I've stopped plugging up my feeling with that kind of explanation. She was memorable. Fiercely memorable. I can't forget her smile. Her profession of love. Her Jane Eee-ree. And as my misery wells up I tell myself other things. I can't leave it alone. I know she is too happy with what she does and with her Jane Eee-ree to ever start wars, cheat people out of their money, snub, back-bite, hold a grudge. A philosopher and sage had the good sense to hire her for that job. On and on I go with the things I tell myself. I know I'm still being condescend-ing, but guilt does that. Not really fair to her. Truth be told, all I really know is what she told me: she loves Jane Eee-ree. That prompts me to offer one last truth:

I have never actually read Jane Eee-ree.

Journal Entries

JULY, 2006

What is today? The 15th? No, the 16th

We gave our second and final performance last night. Good crowds for both performances; most seemed to stay for the whole thing; many positive responses (like we will hear the negative ones...). It was moist and muggy but late enough to miss any direct sun, and we were graced by a number of refreshing breezes, especially last night.

This final week we worked on site, fine tuning. In thinking about it now I would say the final structure was mostly musical (tip: with working with an abstract set of material, think musically). You could call it theme and variations, or a fantasia (that's fan-ta-SEE-ah, please), or even a rondo if you see the theme of return as the actors soaring about between each bit. Talking with Justin (the designer), we decided the story (ah, can't get away from story, can we) of Isaiah, the African boy with AIDS murdered by an outraged uncle, was perhaps the most "integrated" sequence. It had narrative, abstract viewpoints, action, choral echo, use of scenic elements, a riveting culminating image (the narrating actress is covered with a cloth as she "becomes" the body of the dead boy, other actors sediment themselves on top, and then the actress reaches her hand up out of the pile) and a distinct emotional contour with a climax and a coda. But focusing too much on one sequence is to miss the sense of the whole thing and its flow, and we did succeed in maintaining a flow. I also think the piece succeeded in gently coaxing the audience to set aside familiar expectations, to accept just experiencing the unfolding.

How well did it pass what I call the ultimate GHP test? To me the ultimate GHP test (and this tells you too much about my own fears and extreme lack of self-esteem) is: could most of those in the audience, teachers and students, lay aside the natural tendency toward condescension and get caught up in the event? I don't know; too early to tell. Probably you never really know. To a certain extent you hope that the "willing suspension of disbelief" kicks in on its own; you can only lead them to water, after all. I guess I am revealing in part my own battle with condescension toward the kids' approach to the work. And in all honesty, if this truly was a work in progress and we had more time, I don't know what I would want to do. Dale

104

mentioned "more texture," and I would agree, but I am blank at the moment over the question of how to proceed. I would probably have to keep to what Karrie (my teaching partner), Justin, and I have all asserted from the beginning: it's their piece. Does the observation "more texture" have any meaning for them? I would, though, want to get more varieties of text and use of language into the piece, language becoming (the KRAKEN influence coming through) a perpetual "scenic" presence (but not to the extent of ousting those moments of "silence" our actors tell us they love).

There are moments in the piece where surprising and intense encounters between actors emerge in complicated constellations, moments that were originally explored in improvisations and that we were compelled to return to (I was compelled…the kids perhaps were more disbelieving about their worth). Non-narrative moments of emotional weight where the performers let the lines blur between themselves and their "characters." And those are the moments when I feel things are particularly successful, when I got my sensibility across. Two actors forehead to forehead in anger; three actors tearing themselves away from others' ministering actions in a shadowy resolve; an indescribable physical exchange about pizza and macaroni and cheese in which the audience laughs without knowing why; a powerful over-the-shoulder look with deep private significance. Moments where the audience is compelled to attend in spite of their best efforts to condescend.

For those that did not see the performance or for those that cannot get a clear picture from this journal what was going on (I don't blame you), I should try to offer something more, especially if there are some readers who might like to do some of their own group development. First of all, realize that the work can really take any form; a great deal depends on how much time is available for development, the age and temperament of the actors, and on other "teaching goals." We had five weeks to realize a piece, rehearsing two hours an evening Sunday through Thursday up until the last week, and always we had to keep in our minds that the result, our "work in progress," had to be something that accurately reflected the kids' effort and sensibility. Trying to get tricky and make it more sophisticated than it is is always a temptation; we avoid it. The audience came upon the actors moving in a circle which soon dispersed as two actresses began trying to ask their fellow actors "Where is it? What is it?" The actors began to wander about our public space, finally plopping down all over with a provocative gesture of tired indifference. Two actors move across the space as if it's a dry desert; rain finally arrives, the sounds provided by other actors. Two sheets of cloth are undulated over one of the actors, creating a loud troublesome storm, and he cries out, "Pain is life." Actors soar about the space always only three at a time… they then move through a number of sequences which vary in style and mood; there's a search in a library, the Africa story, poetry and monologues, transformations in a playground, a toddler who learns to walk and dance, a traffic accident, fights, moments of personal conflict, a grace lesson…The strips of cloth provide constant shifting "drawings" of atmosphere. One actor plays a didjeridoo (can't remember how to spell it); another punctuates with a djembe. The actors wore comfortable casual clothes in cool colors, each wearing a bit of grey cloth somewhere to help unify the approach. Everything was done through movement and physicality. No props (one notebook and one camera for one scene). Not as much collective vocalizing as I would have liked; some street sounds, a singing of the last verse of Amazing Grace, some humming.

Spoke with one of the actors today. He told me he had had two conversations with people who were "profoundly moved" by the performance. I think there will be more of that kind of conversation between actors and acquaintances who saw it.

Remember, it doesn't have to look like anything you already know. I tell the kids we are going for something *sui generis*, a performance event which may have no precedent. You decide how much the audience needs to know at every instant. The hardest part is getting the kids to relax and not over-explain as part of what they offer. They are in part creating enigmas and unsettling events. The audience will tolerate a certain amount of confusion for the sake of a more powerful payoff down the line. A dream-logic gives you a wide berth and a large canvass and a broad palette. Having said all that, if you want to go instead for a narrative event, by all means do, and it can work at a level of cool Brechtian rationalism if you wish. Just make sure you allow for encounters with the unexpected at some point in the process.

July 8, 2007

The deadline for submitting new material has come and gone, so the next week will be devoted to the actors working on their existing routines, narrowing down the material for the actual production, and finding an interesting way to organize the presentation (order of material, etc). I'm not sure how the organizing will happen this year; probably through a company meeting at which we stare at the charts listing our material. And things will change, of course, once we start running sequences. There's still quite a bit of practical stuff to do: collecting props, building scenic elements for the space, deciding about costume pieces and lobby installations, making arrangements for live music, etc. We begin every rehearsal with a production meeting, and this upcoming week we will devote some class time to rehearsals and such.

I've introduced half the students to "breakout/breakdown" using "The Sick Rose." That group has also had its show session from which they had a recapitulation session to move them toward making a short performance piece. Yes, the freedom they have in the "show" session is quite unbelievable to them. They keep looking over at me like I'm the parent who will sooner or later break up the session because they are *clearly* misbehaving. I remind them of the suggestions I gave them at the beginning and privately enjoy their stupid floundering, which could have been avoided if they had actually listened to me for the last four weeks and kept the materials I gave them. Perhaps even though I speak of opportunities rather than limits, they stubbornly interpret differently. Who knows? I'm afraid it triggers a bit of grumpiness in me. They act like I'm trying to take away their precious playground toys. It wasn't a bad show session, actually, and included some more serious emotional material which may, of course, have been a secret-weapon style stunt on the part of the actress, but may also have been a genuine addressing of a particular emotional terrain inspired by the poem, including a take on the loss of innocence.

July 10

We gave the task of coming up with an order for our routines to a small group of enterprising students (like last year) and the job was completed with no fuss. We ran the order, made some adjustments, and then had a notes session in which all company members were invited to give notes. This is an essential part of the process. I emphasize this as an essential aspect because I believe you need to experience the very things which the more faint of heart would as soon avoid. The kids need to hear the good ideas with the bad so they can start to soberly distinguish between the two. The kids pretty quickly start to understand what it means to listen, really listen, to one another. We want a collision of taste and viewpoint among the members. It's only in sensitively hashing those things out that they learn anything. In fact, often if I don't hear an opposing view voiced on a matter, I will voice it. I want decisions, all decisions, to be creatively challenging and difficult.

If I feel a void in imaginative engagement, I jump in with ideas. If you are feeling fertile, you need to be fertile and chime in. Those that care, do. Those that care more about their own position within the game also chime in, but the kids get to learn the difference between artists trying to serve the piece and kids just wanting to say their piece. I, for one, felt quite energized after the session because I had all my energy focused on the work and was left with a feeling of boundless reserves left over. It felt great to play with ideas and make suggestions. It is a very reflective process, or should be, for us as a group; it is, as reflective as it is, part of the essence of the creative group process–a playful thinking through of what we have.

108

Fording a New Stream: *To ape, he or she aped, I'm aping*

I've found a new stream and invite any and all to play in it.

Yesterday, I was remembering a conversation I had with a teacher a number of years ago and thinking about using it as the basis of a possible article or essay entitled something like *Ideology, Theory, and Creative Intuition*. Juicy title, eh? I will withhold for the present the subject of this conversation (wait and read the article; means I have to really write it), but I can say that as I was recollecting it and mentally rehearsing it and trying to mine it for its usefulness in helping me compose the essay, I had the thought: *this conversation was truly one of the defining moments in my career as an intellectual and artistic ape*. And this observation (more like a confession, really) began to feel as pertinent to the topic I was contemplating as the remembered conversation itself because I was thinking about ideology, theory, and creative intuition not in any general sense, but as they operate in the theatre.

Now let me set that chunk of indulgence aside and get to my point for this post. I like this idea of *The Ape*. And it allows me to think about something I've always wanted to attempt: the performance essay. I'm imagining an essay presented as a performance. The subject of the essay would be an ape running amok in various worlds of arts and letters and in assorted intellectual forums. Aping, to me, is copying, imitating, monkey-see and monkey-do. An easy subject to explore in the theatre and in a performance-based form, it seems to me. And for me, to be serious for only one brief final moment (because thoughts of The Ape cannot remain serious for too long), the basic question I ask myself about The Ape is: Is aping the necessary first step on the road to some authentic embodiment or position (a developmental or evolutionary stage) or just ever-empty display of deficiency that only merits our scorn, laughter or tears as the case may be?

So there's the stream. We play in it and see where it might lead us. The beginnings of a performance essay? We can go anywhere at this point. No rules, just splashing…

Here's a template for creating accounts of meetings which did not take place:

We began on time with everyone in attendance, though _____ came thirty minutes late, missing warm-ups, and _____ left early in order to_____. One stranger was in attendance; _____ never identified _____-self.

_____ led us through a warm-up of _____, some back flips, _____ with and without the bamboo poles, _____, a few arias, _____, and a circle massage. A short session of hypertropic breathing caused _____ to hallucinate, briefly, a _____, entertaining everyone.

110 _____ brought in a new version of_____. This one was shorter by about _____ minutes and did not include the_____ or filling _____'s mouth with rose petals. _____ chose a piece of the new text:

(insert piece of text here)

and while exploring it with _____ managed to conjure up a _____, accented by a spray of _____, ending in a convulsive _____. Upon reflection _____ noticed that the _____ was perfect for the _____ which came after the _____. Then _____, _____, and _____ began repeating a _____ that had appeared during warm-ups. It led to _____ becoming a _____ who was convinced that _____. _____ was reminded of a recent installation described in yesterday's edition of the Times. _____ pointed out that we didn't have to tie up the _____ the way the New York thing did. Everyone agreed.

Then the unidentified stranger offered the observation that _____. This surprised everyone and prompted _____ to attempt to do the entire part about _____ backwards and with _____ poised below _____. Everyone was quite intrigued.

As we concluded _____ suggested we spend more time next week on _____. _____ promised to bring in more _____. _____ made a short comment abou _____ and confessed that it was a source of great anxiety when all was said and done. _____ reminded _____ that nothing was set in stone at this point. In good spirits, we all left and went to _____ for drinks and snacks.

The Writer in Collaborative Group Process

Somebody is bound to be in the room fulfilling a literary function. It might be Shakespeare, of course. Once again I cite KRAKEN as a first inspiration. *Crooked Eclipses* is a work based on the Sonnets; *Elsinore* uses *Hamlet*. More often than not, however, group members assume the writerly roles as they watch and perform, perhaps collaborating with Shakespeare or some other esteemed author or generating their own original material. Below you will find some suggestions for fulfilling the writer's function, and please indulge me as I offer examples from my own attempts.

Engaging with Text Any author can be in the room. It would be an interesting experiment for a group to memorize a play in its entirety, every performer knowing every part, work out a general staging scheme, and then cast a performance by drawing lots five minutes beforehand, with a new drawing before each subsequent performance. The next experiment could involve the group using the text of that play, which it would know inside and out by this point, as its working vocabulary for creating a new piece of performance. Any piece of literature could serve, of course. And it makes sense for another writer to be in the room attempting to chart the adventure. This engagement with pre-existing literary or other textual work is an established technique, I realize. But someone might be reading this who hadn't entertained the possibility. (Look into the Wooster Group's adventures "collaborating" with Arthur Miller; he was not a willing participant and was not happy. Things can get treacherous where living authors are concerned.)

112

Writing as a Response For a writer engaged in producing original work as a part of group process, often in response to what performers may be doing, it may not be as crucial to determine what should be written as how and when to employ it. My first year teaching at GHP, we did not set out to make a company created work. Actor improvisations in class were very inspiring and creative, and it simply seemed a shame not to find a way to show some of the results to a wider audience by, perhaps, weaving the work together in some way. My involvement as a writer that year came about as the result of my teaching partner musing, "there could be something here having to do with the course of a life." In response to that I did not find myself writing dialogue or description or narrative; rather, I began musing, "all of this youthful creative energy ready to emerge into identity…" I had Lacan on the brain in those days, so I began producing what I thought were lyrical Lacanian sentences, trying to think of something that might help weave. I recently found one page of the original stuff:

love is giving what you do not have.

There is a closing hole my name holds open. There is a place where the picture cannot see itself. One day we see something else. And I don't see myself seeing myself see something else. I don't know what I see. I ask. The second question. I ask and I do not give an answer. I ask. I am a question. To have a name means to have a question. And now the world gets very large. One 360 degree wraparound surround. With a hole in the middle.

They will never forgive you for taking the child from them. They will never forgive you. And then you turn around and its gone. Losing sight of something so precious. In such an absence the world ends. But when the world ends you start to see what is behind it. They will turn away. But they will turn away to go their way. Dragging you after. Wanting you bearing witness. Someone to look at the portrait. Don't look. Whatever you do, don't look back.

So many years learning to see yourself. Only to learn that you really need to see something else. Or that you need to close your eyes. Listen. Listen to everything. What he said. What she said. Hear the roads in what she said. Hear the birth in hearing. Time to be born. Time to let yourself be born. Let yourself be born away. What is she saying?

Always before death. You are before death.

No longer asking what I would do were I the one. No longer asking. No past asking. No future asking what would have been. Just the ask. Just ask. I ask. No questioning. No hesitation. No search for the one who will. We all ask. We all will. We will. Just believe it. No names. One name, maybe. No eyes. No I. Maybe an I. Maybe something happening now. As you ask. Something new. Something born. Something to show. Something to do. Before. Before the I. Before the act. Something created. I made it myself.

A bit ponderous, perhaps. Often the performers will supply the wit lacking in the words as they work. At any rate, there would come times in our work where actors would be scattered about the space and feeling an urge to say something. So they would get a scrap of paper from me. Say this. They figured out how to break it up, to score it. And they were good about not worrying too much about what it meant, tuning in, instead, to how the words helped them shape the moment.

Thinking and Observing For a while that first year at GHP, before my teaching partner and I joined forces for one piece, I had a group a kids who were going to invite Shakespeare into the room by taking a look at *King Lear* and creating some kind of work in conversation with the text. My writerly role early in that process was one of memo-writer (memography?):

Notes on performance piece: what's coming up...

I hope after our experiences today (Wednesday) you have some idea about how I am inviting you to work. Starting on Monday, this is how we will work and assemble material; it's a frame in which anything can happen from scene and monologue exploration to surrealist experiments to moments of enigmatic encounter. There is no proper or improper decorum to follow as long as you stay within the work frame and agree to "perform" everything. Bring everything into it. Remember: we will work this way for our audience for about thirty minutes after we do our piece; I will be there prompting you to contribute if I have to. (I hope I don't: it will be much more impressive for the audience to see you totally group driven.)

Now, perhaps, you have an idea why I gave you the hand out on "responding" and on "composing." These are methods we will use. Get familiar with them. What helps me: put yourself into the circle imaginatively and see yourself exploring the strategies with your peers. It helps.

Thursday night we will share our discoveries about the play and the choices artists have made. I will suggest various scenes, encounters between characters, that you are to go off and investigate for further work. Which one interests you? Keep asking yourself what characters and moments in the play you are provoked to explore or shun. We will be transforming YOUR INVESTIGATIONS into a performance piece.

We have started exploring the physical work in the mornings so that you will have things to try with the vocal sequence when you encounter other actors. I invite you to seek out partners and begin exploring on your own and develop a method: one the allows for continual movement and transformation, etc.

Our scenic and costume designers will be joining us and participating as watchers and collaborators.

Fool file: start a list of things the fool says that you like.

Stone and ruin are two ideas that I keep coming back to as I think about the play and talk to the designers. Why do you as a group keep returning to the story of Lear (imaginatively speak-

ing, not "because we're told to")? Perhaps, as painful as it is, you are trying to summon up things to see and experience in order to stay alive. To story yourself into a meaning. Did the end of Lear mean a loss of our center, our system for meaning and being human. You are perpetually crawling out of an impending catatonia, you are resisting turning to stone and ruin, picking through the rubble of form and memory to find a meaning, a consistency. You are caught between NATURE and NOTHING, as are many of the characters in the play. And what does nature hold if our "human" center is lost? Maybe something more horrible than ceaseless predation and copulation, since we need some memory of our humanity to even know the pleasures and horrors of that. Maybe a silent, stony nothing.

I saw many possibilities for exploring the madness in the play as you worked through the sequence. In the play, madness very much is a way to communicate a wisdom that cannot be articulated any other way. But it is also part of the dissolution, the falling apart of order and human decency. Nice paradox.

Friday night we will try to read through the whole play. Keep up the good work.

And here's a bit more:

Notebooks: Please use them. Please, To keep track of what is happening, to remember. One of your jobs is to find ways to perform your remembrances of the play and our work. I may ask you to pick something from your sketchbook to insert at a certain point in the piece, your choice, and I may want you to teach it to several people. Sometimes it will be our thoughtful equivalent of "filling dead air."

Begin collecting phrases from the play and from your thoughts that resonate for you or that reflect thoughts which emerge in the work (you can use strategies like "taking out of context" or "association.") We will use lists of such phrases to create spoken mindscapes or sounded environments.

An actor brings focus, commitment, imagination, strong feeling, and "blooded thought" (phrase from Wallace Stevens). Believe in your ability to make a contribution to this effort. You may never have done this kind of thing before, you may have no interest in doing it again, that is okay. For now, just give yourself over to imagination. GIVE YOURSELF PERMISSION TO PLAY.

THE SINGLE MOST ESSENTIAL THING ABOUT WHAT WE WILL BE DOING AND WHAT MAKES IT UNIQUE: If nothing else, remember: We are going to use the play text to help us find ways to explore what is happening to us in the group. We will use the play to talk about ourselves. The play is like a diving board that will allow us to go into our depths. And who knows what we may finds there.

As you go through the play and note things you like and make you uneasy, ask yourself, Why? Your answer is part of the secret kernel you bring to the work. Protect it. Use it. Explore it.

Director's Initial statement. King Lear is a vast poetic and dramatic landscape. How can we focus our interests so that we can produce a interesting piece within the brief time we have? The last few lines of the play:

The weight of this sad time we must obey; Speak what we feel, now what we ought to say. The oldest hath borne most: we that are young Shall never see so much, nor live so long.

What does this mean for us, and do we believe it? I like the way it seems to make an effort to merge the personal and the political into a kind of mournful ethic. We don't have the time to deal explicitly with the political dimensions of the play (at least, I'm saying we don't), but in many ways our more personal explorations will, to be prompted by these lines, become political .

Clearly in these memos I'm trying to wear a number of hats at once. And this was early in the process. I was using writing to provoke thought and atmosphere and to suggest strategy. Had we continued with this process, my memos would have begun offering thoughts inspired by specific events

116 taking place in group work. Here's a meditation from last summer; often writing is done when I feel powerless to do anything else. We were wrestling with the theme of grace:

Thoughts and opinions on the nature of our performance

Acts of grace. States of grace. Moments of grace. Let's ask, for whom?

For the people in our audience, perhaps. What if we think that it is possible for our audience members to have experiences of grace at our performance?

I think our rehearsals have been, in part, a kind of research in which we have tried to find ways to describe the living qualities of this phenomenon we are calling grace and to understand the types of conditions under which it might occur.

One thing we hit upon was the idea that grace can be something unexpected, taking us by surprise. Consider the experience of our audience: already they will be in a situation ripe for the appearance of grace simply because they will witness our performance in an unexpected place. Even more unexpected: what if they gather at a distant spot on campus and are then led to our location? Suddenly they see in the distance: you, the performers, are walking the perimeter of the stone circle, evenly spaced and in unison of motion. Unexpected place and unexpected event filled with unexpected beauty. There's a silent energy of expectation and they discover that if they choose they can be a witness to…something.

What might happen with this moving circle? Does the audience get closer and discover that each of you is quietly speaking while you walk? Is each of you uttering something different or is your unison of speech as precise as your unison of motion?

How then do we multiply the possibilities for these separate souls in our audience to encounter grace as we act in their midst? What do they see and hear, and witness, and where? What becomes of this circle, this ring of potential energy?

We want to work in ways, I think, that are as present and as determined as the world we see around us. Each audience member will come to the event as an individual, each playing a part in a unique unfolding story, each with a potential to experience our acts and weave their effects into the fabric of his or her own story. We offer the possibility of a kind of collision between their lives and what the world around them is professing (or withholding).

When we think grace has touched us, how does the world around us appear? Are there triggers, patterns, motion, voices, faces?

At that moment, what surrounds us speaks without effort; it is not in the least didactic (not trying to instruct us or impart a lesson). It is too raw and immediate for that; it's as if the world (perhaps through God)

hears minds or our hearts and offers a resonating mystery as a response. We need to remember it is the audience who is to have the experience, and it is for us to offer jarring mysteries and flashes of light rather than instructive stories or illustrations. We want to feed their potential experiences, not presume to be the experience itself.

We don't present the story; we find a way to enact or embody what flashes forth and propels a story (an audience member's story) down a new street. In what ways can we prod them toward an experience of seeing everything differently?

So again, I think both our "theme" and our location will contribute to a very different performance event.

Another result of our research led us to the possibilities for finding grace through children. What is it about seeing and hearing children that can often set the stage for a moment of grace? For me, in a nutshell: children are not actors. They are the thing itself. Their actions are not full of informative built-in annotations designed to explain their meaning or significance. They're never "waiting to go on." They're just on. They do. They just are (to us, the viewer). They're tunes we enjoy picking up and whistling or humming for no particular reason. Often our amazement comes watching them at their most inexplicable. The child utters the surprising remark. The two children engage in some strange dance with a private significance or with no shared significance. Our audience, I think, must experience our work the way one can delight in the actions of children. Which does not mean we should play our piece throughout as if we are young children. No, don't misunderstand me. Then we would just be another group of actors acting like children (and I think the work you have done so far playing young children is far more sensitive and revealing than a simple acting game or exercise, it's a different creature altogether). I'm trying to convey a subtle point about our performance: that it should be as real and self-evident and unpretentious from beginning to end as the truth of children. We live the score of our work completely from start to finish, no gaps, no waits. Almost as if it is a fluid series of ritual actions, precise actions that can at times be very intense and riveting for our audience but are completely empty of show biz or actorly accomplishment. Unless, of course, a bit of show biz is being offered as something for the audience to experience at some particular moment. But then you move on to the next thing, the next act of possibility.

118 *These are just few suggestions inspired by our work together so far. Note they only address form and style, not content. The content is wholly yours.*

I hold no illusions that these words are taken up by the performers as so many pearls dropping from my lips. Often it is the case, as it was with the grace group, that they will be provoked and annoyed by the droning words (I chose to read it at a rehearsal) and go to some new places, as the actors did in this case with wonderful results. Serendipitously, they reacted to my pretentiousness by becoming childish and playful right before I began reading the passage about children. Beautiful happenstance.

Naming Obsessive note taking has been a trait of mine while working as a performer or a creative watcher. The resulting notes are never meant to be a comprehensive transcription, however. Just a record of my own particular attending. The more instances of subjective note-taking, to my mind, the better. Often I share phrases from my notes when the group is in the process of naming something that has occurred, or re-occurred, for "filing" purposes. Others do, as well, as we debate what is the most appropriate name for the phenomenon in question. These attempts at naming in my notes become useful later as ways to spark our memories, inviting us to revisit something we might have been on the verge of forgetting or discounting. Often the names also make for interesting poetic text. The names return not just as memories but words in the performers' mouths or invitations for new actions. One year at GHP our subject was folktales. Here's a listing of names which accumulated during our development:

IT WAS NOT SO LURE THE SNAKE TYRANT KING SHROUDED IN BLACK NO…WAIT BLUE JACKAL BLOWS THEM ALL AWAY DEPARTS FROM LIFE BE BOLD BE BOLD BUT NOT TOO BOLD LAUGH FUNNY TALKING TO BIRDS REAL FRIEND DEMON YOU'RE SHORT FAMILY OF BRUTES HOW LOVELY TWO LOVERS CAREFREE SAGE THE EYE IS DEATH EVIL GIVE US A TASK OR WE WILL KILL YOU WHERE THE EARTH MEETS THE SKY A SWALLOW THINGS SEEM BRIGHTER ON THE OTHER SIDE BIRD AND SKULL GOD HELPS THOSE WHO HELP THEMSELVES DO SOMETHING NOW AROSE EVIL CHILD PASSION NO, NO THE SEA'S CRAZY MUSTARD SEED SWEEPING THE FLOOR AND SHE TURNED INTO A FOX ONE IN ITS DESTINY A SQUIRE A CHAMELEON THAT WAS THE END OF THAT SHADOW IN THE EYE FALLS AND SPLITS IN TWO AND SHE TURNED SPIRIT IS ONE MOON FIRST LIVED AT THE BOTTOM OF THE SEA SELLS HIS SOUL CANNOT BE BORN AGAIN LIVED IN THE SEA LOOKING FOR A PLACE WHERE MEN DO NOT EAT OTHER MEN THE FATHER'S GRAVE EARTH AND SKY SURROUNDED BY MINIONS HE COOKED IT AND HE ATE IT NO COOKING NO EATING LORD YOUR GOD DECIDES TO MARRY TWO BROTHERS PREGNANT GOAT NOBODY KNOWS BUT ME BUT I KNOW COME INSIDE THIS INSTANT GETTING CLOSER SOMEONE HAS STOLEN MY HAMMER HAUNTED ROOM GOT YOU WHERE I WANT YOU NOW I'M GONNA TWO POTS ONCE LONG AGO RICH MAN ELEGANT WIFE WE THE JURY OF THE JUNGLE IN PERU THE BOY WHO HORSE AND ASS STUPID SON AND THEY SET OFF THEN LET THEM BE TOWN AND RIVER BONE PALACE FLOUR TIN CHANT WE ARE THE HUMBLE WRAPPED IN BUGS BIRDS AND BEASTS A BONE STUCK IN HIS THROAT THE WOLF THE SNAKE AND THE LIGHT WENT ON AND SHE WAS CALLED THE FATTEST OF ALL SHE CRUSHED THE LITTLE LIZARD FOLLOW ME WHAT JOURNEY NOBODY CARES FOR ME SHRINKING INTO STONES THY WILL BE DONE I'M DONE ALL IS ONE OLD FOLKS SUN AND THE MOON A PRINCESS EVIL EYE

119

Just in the reading, for me, a kaleidoscopic delirium is at play and calling out for some attempt at performance. As a map of memories, it also charts the collective dreams of the group. Here's one from this past summer's work on the theme of grace:

STRUCTURE OF A PILGRIMAGE. WORDS OF A SWIM COACH. SAYING GRACE. BEING GIVEN SOMETHING POWERFUL. CHORAL EFFECTS. FASCIST INTO DANCING LEPRECHAUN. A DAY'S GRACE. BEFORE IT GETS DARK. TOO BEAUTIFUL FOR WORDS. OMNI-PRESENT. 14,000 TONGUES. GRACE AND JOY TILL THE END. FLOWER STRUGGLING. TIME RELEASED POWER. RESTRAINING POWER. FATHERS AND FORGIVENESS. GRACEFUL OLD LADIES. OVERCOMING. IMPERFECTIONS. BABIES. EASE AND POWER OF CERTAIN BEINGS. CRAP. THE FED EX GUY. THE DANCE OF THE TWO APPEARING RAINBOWS. SEEING THE FACE WHILE HE SWIMS THE BACKSTROKE. COTILLION GIRL WITH BOOK ON HEAD. IT CAN'T BE FOUND; IT FINDS YOU. BETTER AS A MYSTERY. POINTING TO HER TOES. ALL WAYS GRACE. THE SURVEY (TO ASK AND TO SEE). FINDING IT BY LETTING GO. MOMENTS TO LIVE OVER. SCRIPTURE. HEARTS WITH WINDOWS. HOLE IN MY CHEST AND THE WIND GOES RIGHT THROUGH. HAP. THE WORD ITSELF. MERCY. REVEAL AND CONCEAL. SAVING GRACE IN THEATRE. SOMETHING THAT FLOWS. SEEING IT. WHAT YOU LOVE. SEEING SOMETHING UNIQUE. FINDING YOUR OWN LANGUAGE. KIDS LEARNING TO WALK AND DANCE. SHARED TENSION BEFORE THE FALL. THE THREE GRACES. MEMORY. LACK OF GRACE, LACK OF WORD, LACK....GOD'S MADNESS. REINCARNATION OF A MOMENT. WHAT ARE WE SEARCHING FOR. COMING FROM UNEXPECTED PLACES. COMING FROM OUTSIDE RITUAL. I AM NOT SICK. NIGHT PRAYERS. GRACE STATION. SLOPPY SLUGGISH SLOGANEERING. ATMOSPHERE OF A FUNERAL WITHOUT A CORPSE. WHERE'S GRACE, SHE'S SUPPOSED TO DANCE. GOOD GOING, GRACE. HEARTBEAT OF GRACE. CIRCLE OF LIFE. RING AROUND THE ROSY. DANTE'S INFERNO. DOWN THE RABBIT HOLE. FROM THE STREET TO THE LIBRARY; FROM THE LIBRARY TO THE STREET. GRANDMA VARIATIONS. NIGHT SOUNDS. DARK SECRET LOVE, SHH. THREE MOTHER; THREE DAUGHTERS; THREE QUESTIONS. THE ATHEIST FAMILY. THE COOKIE RECIPE. LITTLE RINGS REVEALING GRACE.

More titular in spirit perhaps and not as surreal, but still evocative.

Research The writer often can infect the performers with a craving for bookish investigation. The goal is for everyone to start haunting the stacks at the library as questions emerge during rehearsal. The writer begins, often, by bringing in words, facts, arcana, material charged with occult energy. Alchemical ingredients. Our work on the grace piece led me to expressions of Christian mysticism. I would offer the results of my explorations to the group:

texts and notions reflecting the mystical outlook:

from The Mirror of Simple Souls *by Marguerite Porete, first heretic burned to death in the Paris inquisition, June 1, 1310. Porete was considered a Beguine: "They read Scriptures irreverently, audaciously in coventicles, street corners, and public squares."*

I had copied out by hand and by Xerox pages from Ellen Babinsky's rapturous translation...

Such a soul, said Love, swims in the sea of joy...She feels no joy, for she herself is joy, and swims and floats in joy without feeling any joy, for she inhabits joy and joy inhabits her.

And on and on. Porete had also formulated a "Seven States of Grace" which felt like a possible way to structure things. I flooded them with Porete's amazing outpourings of ecstatic confession. My other big find for the grace work was Pseudo-Dionysius:

Pseudo-Dionysius on Apophasis and Mystical Knowledge

Breaking hold of Reason upon the soul through negation, paradox and contradiction

Here I pulled from a translation by Paul Rorem. Phrases that exploded.

Reason and Will die

A soul who lives without a why

Darkness of unknowing

Brilliant darkness of a hidden silence

Amid the wholly unsensed and unseen, they completely fill our sightless minds with treasures beyond all beauty

I would offer these findings as potentially useful to the mix, but there are no guarantees. If performers take them up in some way, great. If you want them to take them up, you may have do some work as an advocate. As a writer, I could not just shake off the material; it began to re-appear in some of the poetry I wrote in response to the group's work, serving as textual seeds for ideas or as found artifacts. We ultimately did not structure our work upon Porete's seven states of grace, but all discoveries and words leave traces.

Group Process as Writing, Writing as Arranging: More "memos" to the grace group:

Simple recipe for making performance art:

1. Raid your memory archive.

2. Re-incarnate the moment.

3. Contemplate it in stillness.

4. Animate it.

5. Find ways for it to breathe with life and expression.

6. Subject it to variation. Add, subtract, multiply, divide.

7. Think about impact.

8. Compose it for virtuosos; strip away excess; take away scaffolding.

9. Could a hack script it? If so, discard.

10. Does it scream a message? If so, discard.

11. Are you left with a sense of "it is what it is?" If so, it is successful.

Try to put together at least one moment that will baffle your peers. Work with tiny pieces.

122

How to create original text for a performance piece, suitable for any uttering actors or group choral orchestration or other enigmatic exchanges:

1. Go through your notes.

2. Pick expressions from various pages, no order.

3. You can put them on separate pieces of paper and then draw them from a hat.

4. Or you can shuffle them on the page.

5. Good syntax (sentence construction) is not necessary.

6. Let sensation and a desire for musical experimentation be your guides:

...encouraging kisses....everyone else hidden...father child... ranting ravings everything reminds us why...baby to child... mother child...watching conversations and hearing spare questions...around her the same contorting creatures...lifted long enough to see.

7. Or take a page of journal and fold it in, halving the sheet, so that you see half of the page beneath. Read lines across the central crease from the folded page to the underpage (or reversed depending on which way you fold):

She begins with what affliction? The sound takes on grace. Reach-

ing all out sick. It dissipates. Find someone this happened to. A division in courage. Avoiding pictures of the spine and how we move. Just like the lack of place, the grace of the neighborhood. What words take the ends of the spectrum? What are the needs of her central love? Just like the lack lost son showing memory as a violin. God words and dances. A sub-text of sitting, all of a sudden sparkling. You make it the black fear. Shying to do a pirouette. Returning to the dance for her second chance. Girl with book on her graduation. Eye-static and druggy. Dreampeer wordwore usetwobooks to be granted and diagnosed and too beautiful for she doesn't care.

Far in purple

Poetry and Textual Experiments This past summer, the work on our grace piece was pushing me down many a desperate avenue in an effort to find words. The conundrum is pretty clear: how can you put words to something beyond words? I found myself trying to make poetry compiled from images, phrases, and words which were recorded in my journals. I don't know what I thought the group might do with it all. I was nursing a desire to coordinate some complex choral moments or even isolate smaller "scenes" in which the poetry would function as a kind of oblique dialogue. *Tempus fugit:*

123

Grace is always on her toes

 Grace is always on her

Grace is always honor

Graces always honor those (who........)

Happened

To her the word itself happens

Happening to him to them. Happenings

Co-incidence. Happenstance.

Hers is the tick of her toe on the clockface. Louder than the hour itself. His is more like the swinging of the bell in the tower.

Feet planted squarely. Theirs is too small to see,

But it ticks all the same

And me too. And me too. And me too.

It happens and how

how does it happen?

The sweet sound of shedding skin

alone in the dark wood,

leaving it for the wild cats to sniff

escaping through a hole in the pavement.

A maze of grates depletes the ground,

Unsafe for wretches' feet.

Eyes punched, then tossed

Up on a mound,

I'm fine, I'm fine, really...

Steaming up from the slits in the ground and filling the air with sugar and piss. How sweet.

The world is full of evils. Demons beating their own small hearts.

* The rhythms of will be will be will be*

Of my will be done. Charming plays and librettos

And plenty of actors, a whole shelf of them, Adept at manipulation.

Do you remember the movie:

Where they gathered together Where she looked out the window and vanished Where they grew up gracefully And no one was left out And Baroque ceilings left them laughing And there were no questions And by the time they laid us down to sleep

We had proved it in at least seven different ways

Unio mystica

A mating place, how meekly found, That cave was etched

O-R-D-E-T

Do you remember the movie about the miracle?

Do you remember the play with the obscure reference? Can you find grace in a mirror? Hiss your steam on the glass...

That would be considered one sustained outburst. Clearly I was hoping the play on the page could somehow turn into a playing on the stage. Here's another :

Possible title: ...grace...period.

a loan in love

In love she is a swim coach alone

slaking herself in saying with beautiful

chorus effects

and giving nothing knowing no tongue

only time released struggling swimming

with a book balanced on the head. Love draws her up

and the wind isn't blowing through;

only use flows through.

What is the meat of grace? Why has love run down the rabbit hole? On the streets are mad handouts Crap swims in the sea of joy

our habits in the dark fascist dance wearing the habit she feels no joy

her joy only inhabits joy

Love who had so often driven me from the street to the library

Work with a recipe

little images of

God's madness small sloppy rituals old ladies letting go a beautiful solitary phoenix.

I don't want to be a phoenix.

I want to be something learning to walk

Like the corpse at a funereal dance.

I want to learn the rainbow's backstroke.

I want release from restraint.

What to do?

The sky scares me.

Graceless hands reach out of the clouds.

Are these those clouds of unknowing

The books talked about?

125

Am I crossing into wonder? What to do?

I feel so helpless.

All the familiar doctors

Touching the familiar folds

and I quake in the same cold ways. Am I made of water? Why?

In a quest of a language of the unspeakable I found myself getting quite Joycean at some points; I even included a little primer for the group on producing Wakean language:

You, too, can churn out passages of potential performance poetry. Use any aforementioned method; use your texts and found texts. Performance poetry can be performed in any imaginable way. Let it provide a music for mysterious encounters. Let it be the dialogue for soulful conversations or sublime choruses. Place it into a kinetic sculpture.

Mad Handouts: what might we read on a mad handout? Take a slogan or proverb or cliche and warp it in some way. making it say several things at once.

You can also manipulate language to try and speak the unspeakable, using the familiar:

Amazing glaze,

All sweet and brown

You saved the meal for me.

We lunched: we noshed;

It was astound

-ing how much We could eat.

A gaze too late's

our suite's last frown,

A look is lost on me.

I'm dunced; you cost

Too much, compound

-ded now but interest-free.

or making the unfamiliar with the familiar,

   a why in the text try

   a promise of poemis

   a mattering memologue

   a peace of greysoft lowly slowrosy

   the someself as yoursalve

      grand playomancy

      peasposed and tablepoised

      sing and deflinging wings

   empty clumpty sadsank on the shelf

   knottingcootie coats of blue sadbliss

   godofound in holemounts and black

   fistworks mercyhurts and sighterific mystershins

   cuddlady dancingdo in a silly swank cottiline

   speedylicious aspersions and glandscrapes

   gorgeous windseawindows agape-ay

   a quickwink to the campuslink

   uneven ethyr in poorpistule emoantion

   suddenducksdrift sideways sandsordid for everyash and covercash

> *This technique I borrowed from James Joyce in his Wakean mood. Good way to evoke a feeling of a dream language. Or a language of unsaying, maybesaying, a sangwitch of speech scorchery?*

I also tried to push the grace group toward fashioning dialogue through experimental and associative methods. Because so many of the working techniques we were employing, such as the Vocal Sequence, asked the performer to move into some serious extremities of expressive possibility, I tended to favor texts and textual approaches which might crack open and disperse all guarantees of consistent meanings, grammatical consensus, and reasoned discourse. But often, too, you just go where the subject matter seems to be taking you. The "scripts" that follow are not transcripts, just whimsy inspired by a desire to put words into the mouths of performers working at the outer boundaries:

And I couldn't resist. Some suggestions for how to create dialogue using "performance poetry." Scatter some letters out for number and order of speakers and just plug in text.

A: Add to that thought.

B: To that trace.

A: To that history.

C: There's some kind of cancer there.

(pause)

A: Where?

B: Please punch me.

D: Down those dark aisles.

(pause)

B: I'm feeling like memory has left.

D: Without God.

A: Don't say that.

C: Without...

(pause)

B: We're not seeing.

C: Perhaps you want me to be your favor dispenser.

B: Not sparkling anymore.

A: Sorry.

B: You thought I had more to say.

D: My sight.. .is limitless.

A: Your choice of words.

Or, in a more Wakean vein:

A: I'm puffing through mirrorous bad grimories. So many ball brats, so many,

B: You knead more delicious audmissioning, my dear.

A: Singing a song of sixth sense, I uptoes.

B: I uprose so. Co-quenchidentally, you could,

A: Don't wear a couldhood and cahoots with me!

What? You whoyou! What?

C: Peeping like aleaven heaving heaven, priss miss!

B: Poorlaps I should be maptized, baby curl.

C: The cokecan says,

A: You're smelling me up a tree about what the coke-can says.

B: That's allah she wrote, and dearly there his no antic-dope.

A: Making maybe one two many tearful oponions. Two four many players to feel away.

B: And find what next text sub rosa.

C: Mostly.

A: Tear flicks clear nicks steer quicks appearing thick-ly. A toad implores exposed sword chord out to the fiord.

B: The spear is spilling, my sweet, but the flash is meek.

C: And the meek, ma chere, clearly inhibit the mirth.

Or:

  A: There's another circle.

B: Another? Where?

  A: Hidden in this one.

  B: No one is there.

C: Someone is.

B: A child alone.

C: Sewing up images.

B: Into the stone.

A: Whenever there's a lull.

C: A brilliance opens up.

A: A light in the crack.

Or some purgative Vaudeville:

We are unclean.. .Where I come from...We are unclean.. .Where I come from.. .We are,...Where I come from...Yes?.. What?..Well, where you come from...?..Where?... What?.. What where?..What about where you come from?.. Where I come from...we sing!..You sing?..Yes..we sing!... So...we are still unclean...Yes?..We are unclean and sing-ing will not clean us....Singing will not clean us...No.. Singing will not clean us....No.. .Bathing perhaps will clean us.. .Please.. .And singing.. .You are not being se-rious...Where I come from we sing when we bathe...We cannot be cleaned....You, my friend, need to hear me

say a series of words to you...A series of words.... Yes.
Tulip oxygen formaldehyde reach please and thank
you ladybug game level pattern ashtray innocuous
entire porridge wind eat wall ambulance...flower.....Is
that it?...For now, yes.. .Words are crap. They're nothing.
They're noise...

Often in rehearsal you see the actors pushing toward encounters and you watch the words fail, particularly when time is
limited and sensibilities are still a bit young and bewildered; so
much of my writerly contribution, particularly with younger
students, is just trying to model the idea that anything is possible, that communication is a wide and complex undertaking,
particularly in performance work. The actors don't always realize how layered and expressive they are as so many signaling
bodies in space with their eyes attempting to lock onto something not quite available to sight as yet. Many lines of expression are moving simultaneously. Sometimes it is hard for them
to let go of the desire to carry the burden of the meaning all
on their own. It's not always necessary to know exactly who is
speaking or to what end. One more:

A: Lost in a maze of long discussions about sin.

B: I suggest as we sit upon our cold wood
stools and dip our toes into the rising black
water, we take a moment.

A: I don't think I have the time to take that mo-
ment. I would rather go ahead and fall.

B: Falling is easy.

A: Easy for you. You can bleach the streets white with
your last cry for help and believe it will make a dif-
ference.

B: You on the other hand I suppose are too lost to
even offer up a squeak.

A: Look at me. If I could grab hold of something I
would. I would grab hold of God if I felt I had the
strength.

B: If God were a woman...

A: God is a woman.

B: That's your wish for some quiet breath and tears
flowing behind the mad slaughter of human history.

A: The moment I woke up and knew who she was.. .I
finally could feel honored to be unworthy.

Putative Origin of Symmetrical Hand Arrangements

I'm thinking about what happened during the Paris Commune of 1871. A sculpture student at the *École des Arts Plastiques* (the scant enrollment documentation from the *École* for that term referring to him variously as Felix or Felice or Fleece (?!), no surname recorded) responded to the shortage of marble (quarry workers throughout European went on strike in sympathy with the workers in the city) by undertaking what the ever-arch Zola would describe in an article years later as a "ridiculous exercise." *"Exercice ridicule."* Our aspiring student began to spend his studio class time sitting upon a stool in the corner and fashioning a series of formations with his hands that elaborated upon the various *"mirroir identites"* possible through such manipulations. There is one bit of scribbled anecdotal recollection attributed to this enterprising and impoverished visionary, a scrap salvaged from a dustbin, now a thing of legend: "My professors insisted I must occupy my time well while I waited for the meager eighteen cubic centimeter allotment of stone which I was told must last me for the whole month of June. I undertook a study. I began to explore symmetry. And with material in good supply. *Le renouvellement est infiniment.*" "Infinitely renewable."

130

We're able to bring a remorseless, gritty reality to our facial scrub.

Suddenly motionless in the kitchen, he takes a moment to appreciate it's no easier finding the good grater than the greater good.

"Controlling how you share"...indeed. Trying to. Trying...to.

"That was very dry, my dear. Very dry.
You are, no doubt, the driest one here.
Though I'm compelled to ask if you've noticed
the most truly worthwhile pursuits in life
involve a good bit of moisture. (Pause.)
A greasing of the wheel. (Pause.)
A wetting of the whistle. (Pause.)
Finding your way through the primordial
soup. (Pause.)
So where does that leave you? (Pause.)
Really. Where?"

Our roué
sommelier:
"In the finish of this Fumé
You'll detect her hint of 'You May.'"

Since the day of our marriage, if not even some time before, my wife has had a manqué on her back. Keep her in your thoughts and prayers.

This manqué is alway all-too-ready to perform his tricks. You don't even have to turn a crank or feed me peanuts.

the sigh for my self: amen dove, a null assist, poor chance

Breaking Away

This exercise involves a cycle. The second wheel of this cycle was added by the 2003 class.

To do a Breakout means to internalize something you have discovered while performing the Vocal Sequence. In other words, you transform what may be a very extreme vocal, physical and psychological expression into a realistic aspect of a realistic character. So, yes, a Breakout means to take inside. A paradox. And the first wheel of this cycle involves engaging in the Vocal Sequence and moving to a Breakout when asked to do so by one or more watchers. You work with the sequence until someone shouts "Breakout!" At that moment you take your Vocal Sequence "fixation" (a call for "Breakout" implies you have arrived at something interesting) into an expression of a real person, saying real words, following real intentions. This real person should be based on your Vocal Sequence discovery, on some vital rhythm, some psychological *gestalt* of character, some acoustic particularity.

The cycle is complete, gaining a second wheel, when someone shouts "Breakdown!" At that point you return to working with the Vocal Sequence, beginning from wherever you were in your realistic performance. The watchers wait for something newly interesting and call for "Breakout" again. You can ride this Breakout/Breakdown cycle until Breakfast if you so choose.

It can be a bicycle for two. Two can begin working the Sequence, separately or in a mirroring relation, and begin a "scene" when someone calls for the Breakout. A variation on this involves the two performers going into a round of Hysterical Hygeneassist while in Breakout as their new characters.

Could this cycle be for more than two? Try it and see.

(The mysteries of the Symbolic: Originally this section was going to be called "Breakdancing." As I began writing I changed it to "Breaking Away" because the dance reference felt like I was an old geezer trying to hard to connect, not succeeding, not remotely contemporary. The notion of the exercise as a cycle came forward and then the impulse to pun on the two meanings of cycle. Once I began writing I then remembered that Breaking Away was a film from the late Seventies about a teenager who wants to enter the Tour de France, a bicycle race. From a Lacanian psychoanalytic point of view this is an innocent example of the material and signifying nature of the Unconscious. The "cycle" was already contained in the connections to Breaking Away. Or was I thinking about "cycle" in some remote way and, consequently, "Breaking Away" immediately pedaled into view, beating out "Breakdancing" as the somehow more appropriate title though still a "dated" reference; the joke's still on me. In either case, "it" was doing the "thinking" for me. Just show up. If you feel a task is beyond you, sometimes just showing up is still the best thing to do. If you show, "it" will inevitably show you something. Somewhere in that you'll find a key to creative process and an improvisation tip.)

THE ART OF TELLING THE TRUTH

I want us to produce an evening (coffee house-ish, readings-ish) with the above ironic title and based on our work with that exercise. Last night has inspired me to try and create one (prepared, not improvised) and to write some more about ways of using and developing the exercise.

Briefly, for now, the keys for me are in the "existential categories." [Ed. note: time, space, body, objects, and intersubjectivity]

These I stole from existential-phenomenological psychology and various methods it employs to do *qualitative research*. Language, itself, speaking itself, are not categories, their puzzling nature *bracketed*, or set aside, and we assume a person can transparently relate a description of an event. The best modern playwrights, of course, factor in the troubling nature of language and recollection, but you don't always have to. It's a good creative exercise for unfolding the possibilities in dramatic communication. And the fact that the event might have happened but didn't flirts with the whole question of longing or desire or regret (part of our emotional secret as we work with this kind of material; it will fuel the whole production).

134

Everybody, take a shot at the exercise. You can work in solitude. You need not improv it on demand. Soon I will publish some more suggestions as I continue to work with my own material, but for now–

TWO MAIN APPROACHES:

1. Think of the event. Describe it. Go back over the description and do an analysis using the existential categories. Which ones did you feature? Which ones did you neglect? Add to your full description by working through the neglected elements. Did you attend to what your "body" was about in the description? What happens if you do? How did you interact with others (intersubjectivity)?

2. Think of event (both of these approaches involve positing the event at the outset; you could describe your way toward the event, but that's "more advanced," I think, so try one of these approaches first) Write descriptions of the event, one for each existential category (one for time, space, body, object, and for intersubjectivity) You will have five texts. Then experiment with cutting and pasting; combine elements from your five

texts into the final monologue.

Then, ONCE YOU HAVE TAKEN ONE OF THESE AP-PROACHES:

Think through how you want to perform your monologue (it's still you speaking at this point) using the five existential categories; create descriptions based on this exploration, see if additional lines suggest themselves, add them to your piece.

For example, what additional lines might be inspired by your attending to the performance's

- *time*: "My speaking to the listener(s) is timeless; was that only three minutes? I want to dwell a bit longer, to linger, over details."

- *space*: "The listener and I are alone in a room in my parents' house; I'm sitting in an uncomfortable chair (body leaks in here)."

- *body*: "I feel insubstantial, all in my head"

- *object*: "Why am I telling you this, the words are hard to say, but the image is enjoyable, I want to conjure something for the listener, but I'm afraid."

- *intersubjectivity*: "The listener is an old friend but has never heard this story; I worry she will disap-prove."

How does thinking through this way make you want to add to or subtract from your monologue? Does it influence choice of word or detail? Re-work. As you re-write you are also doing your actor's homework.

I'm going to try to compose one using method two by the time of our next meeting. I have to be out of town, but I'll try to send the text along.

Some masterpieces of recollection in which you are unsure of the status of the recollector, i.e., is he/she remembering it correctly or even telling the truth: Beckett's *Krapp's Last Tape*; Pinter's *Old Times* and *Monologue*; Shepard's *Killer's Head*.

mouth to mouth: a monologue

Remember. Eyes closed.

Eyes closed? Now then.

Spent prom night at a cast party. Saturday night. Things started late.

Moving from room to room. Peeking into the ballroom. Yes. A ballroom. Didn't want to be there, though. Didn't want to be seen there.

Local arts matron had this stately mansion. Been there

plenty of times. The party house. Imagine it. Better than a prom. Big stairs in the foyer. Two sets, one on each side. People always sitting. Up and down. Show business.

Okay. Okay. Here goes. Up and down the stairs. Noises in the ballroom. Full of queens on quaaludes. Enough of that. Friend keeps turning the corner. Grinning. Keeps popping up.

"Leave me alone." "She's looking for you." "Yeah." "Go find her." "Yeah."

"She's yours if you go find her." Eyes closed, remember. "She's yours."

That sounds awful, doesn't it. "Yours." If wanted. If wanted. And drunk on top of that. And there for what if wanted. "Go find her."

That kind of party. Cups of beer from the keg. Quaaludes in the ballroom. Business. Busi ness. Running from room to room thinking there's another pot simmering. A third party of all things. Don't want to mess that up. Going to Six Flags tomorrow. Something may come of that.

Not to be dwelt upon. "Just go and find her." Just go. Do something.

Wait. It's getting there. Now then. So no more running away. Turning around. No more reservations. There on the staircase.

There on the staircase. An idiot looks up the stairs. A walking advertisement for Banana Republic looks up the stairs. Panama hat and tropical shirt. Upper buttons open. Give em a glimpse of the man flesh.

There. Up there. Alone on the staircase. No one else present. Rare moment. "Just find her." So now found.

Capri length jeans. Everyone in jeans. Jeans were the thing. White button down oxford. Maybe a blue oxford. Cuffs rolled. Curls of hair hiding the collar.

"She's not going to follow you around. Just find her." What to do now?

Sixteen steps to the second floor. The choice to sit. To climb to the eleventh step and sit. One step below. Looking up to the step above. And on the step above a face that used to seem too large. What was that about?

"I didn't do the dance exactly right tonight." The face

and the voice curling about it. The voice curling and slurring slightly.

"I didn't see it." Seeing. That didn't come out right. And seeing. Something troubling. Unsettling

From the first day in freshman homeroom the face seemed too large. Felt like it was always intruding. But now. It's different.

Maybe it was always meant to be right there.

Maybe that's the wish. Right there.

Patience. Eyes closed. Now,

"I'm glad you didn't see it. I messed up." Leaning back, shoulder against the wall, a step above, face wide and right there.

"I mean I'm always looking for the swords then. I never get to see it. We're on right after the dances."

Were on. Show was over. "We were on after the dances."

Then the face comes forward. There it was. That was the crush. That was the face, too wide, head tilting from side to side and back.

Still too fast. This should take more time. Eyes closed.

Now suddenly running down a sixth grade hallway. Lee Ellen Robideaux running behind in mock slow motion. "Kiss me kiss me kiss me." Very funny. Running from that and hiding in the boys' bathroom. It's not real if it's asked for. It's teasing if it's asked for. Hide and cry. Hate being followed.

Now the eyes are asking something, face smiling and waiting, turning side to side like a doorknob being tested. Quietly.

Give me a moment.

Deciding to look. Deciding to climb the stairs.

First kiss, remember.

Should have been younger. Should have taken less time to get there. Should have and sooner.

Now. Remember. Eyes closed. Then. Mouth. Open. Mouth. Leaning in. To know what leaning in means. Sliding on the staircase. Noise in the ballroom. Together. Knowing it's safe to lean also. Up to the face. Eyes closed. Neck. Bending. Back bending in also. Sixteen steps. Mouth stays. Mouth says kiss me kiss me kiss me. Mouth close. Mouth open. Drinking in beer and

toothpaste. Resting against the wall. Tilting down. Start-
ing and finishing. Beer and toothpaste and a touch of
something acid underneath. Pulling away to look. Eyes
open. Eyes closed. Going back to the acid. The acid's
the best part. Crying in the ballroom. Figuring out how
it turns into making out. Arm out to touch a shoulder.
All of a sudden. Climbing up a step. Hand down brac-
ing on a knee. Breath and contortion. All of a sudden.
Neck bent. Mouth.

Then pulling back again.

Not yet. Eyes still closed.

Looking one step up. Looking as if to say smiling as if
to say

"It's fine. Isn't it."

A touch of spit by the lower lip.

To kiss and disappear. Trying to smile and not hate the
thing in the mirror. Smile. It will be fine. It's fine. Wipe
it away.

A touch of spit, a drop.

Reach out and wipe it away. Trying to seem confident.
Smile and wipe both sets of lips. Make it a joke.

Try to really be there, really there, a step below,
close, alone with both.

A little more time. Just a moment. Eyes closed.
Still.

Wait.

Mouth reaching back in. Leaning in again.

Now then. Just for you.

I she my her me I she mine I hers you she me I she mine
her I you she

she her mine I me you she hers she I she she

Okay. That's it. Eyes open.

Done.

Acting: the first four fundamental lessons

I

An actress did not receive any notes from me after the first dress rehearsal. She approached as we were adjourning. Anything for me? I remember sputtering and stuttering. Let me note immediately that she was a talented and capable performer. I could have, if nothing else, offered something about what I liked in her performance. So what if I didn't have to have a brilliant insight into what she might be lacking at that moment? What was my problem? I told her something that would somehow cover over the fact that I had nothing. First dress and she's hungry for a response, a reaction. I knew that this was a moment where, as a director, I had a fundamental responsibility. It was a basic test, and I had failed utterly. And I knew it immediately. It was with great and miserable relief that I retreated into the darkened auditorium.

Step back a few months to my first meeting with the costume designer. The play was a period costume piece--Europe in the early nineteenth century--and a studied look at the Romanticism of that era. We discussed the style of women's dress, particularly the high Empire waist and more particularly the low necklines above those Empire waists. We were having a jolly time. The spirit of the play and the era should also be expressed in a certain forthright eroticism in our choice of fashion. She goes on to tell me that often the dresses were sprayed with water to cause the fabric to cling to the flesh and leading to more than a few fatal cases of pneumonia. Wet dresses, we agree, might be going too far. But the necklines, yes, there we will go.

And I don't remember if I had already more or less cast the play at that point. I want to believe that I had. I must believe that I had. If I had not, then I am a despicable grub worm. I am lower than low. Once the costume designer invoked the image of the neckline, I began to think about actresses with *endowments*. Corruption was instantaneous and absolute and I lost certainly about everything, even time. So had I in fact already cast it? I came to believe my interest in necklines reached back in time, already at work even before it became an explicit issue in discussions with the costume designer. I had probably already been thinking about it from the moment I thought about doing the play. So I am a loathsome entity. I was from the get-go. There was no before. No matter what I may have believed I was thinking about the talents and abilities of particular actresses I knew (it was school, so everyone knew everyone) and about whether or not they might be right for the assorted roles in the play, what I was thinking in actuality was: *talented* and *endowed*. My guilty appetite shaped everything.

Back to the first dress rehearsal. I am sitting in the dark and seeing, suddenly, how it is all so realized. I feed greedily. Talent/endowment. It is shameful and delightful. I am not a director taking notes. I am not reflecting. I am content. I lack nothing. And the actress who will approach me afterwards with her doubt, her questions? She isn't lacking anything, either.

II

The woman at this particular restaurant works as the hostess but also clearly presides as the owner. Every time I go there I ponder my discomfort. She is not exactly unwelcoming, but I always do feel that she is slightly put-out with the fact that it is I and not someone else more suitable who has turned up to occupy a table. Even when I've made a reservation.

140 Once it had been decided that one of the roles I'd be playing in an all-male production of *Coriolanus* was Volumnia, Coriolanus's mother, I immediately thought about this woman at the restaurant, this woman who clearly ruled, who was right, who I would never please. And who would eagerly turn one of her recently sacrificed and butchered children into the special of the day. Something about the incongruity of a skeletal woman running a restaurant. There was a different sort of feeding at work.

There would be no costume or make-up changes as I jumped among roles in this production, so I had to come up with something more immediate, ceremonial, and emblematic. This woman at the restaurant wore a chain around her neck with a pendant hanging from it. I am certain it had seen it around her neck each time I'd been there. It was part of her. This, then, would be the way I would become Volumnia. Just put on the chain with the pendant. The bauble. When I wear it, I have the power.

The nature of the power? I don't know. I went to Goodwill to look for something that might work. A chain with a thing dangling. What might it betoken? Her disgust? How might you get her to see you as valuable rather than as noxious? A second-hand store: the place where one person's trash becomes another person's treasure. How might you be transformed into a treasure in her eyes? Only by sacrifice.

III

Another earlier stripped-down production of Shakespeare with a small cast handling all of the roles: *As You Like It*, this time. I played Orlando, Charles the Wrestler (so I had to wrestle myself), the country wench Audrey, and assorted Lords. The production received press coverage, and even though I was generally ambivalent about acting, having done no more than stumbled and fallen into a few roles up to that point, I found myself evaluated, the critic deploying a couple of choice phrases. I had been reviewed. It was no longer possible to hide behind ambivalence. Things were writ down now. I had to make some decisions about what the hell I was doing.

Obvious comic gifts but lacking vocal interest. Such was the reviewer's verdict. Let me address the "comic gifts" thing first. When you are required to wrestle yourself, it's kind of a prepackaged comedic tour de force slam-dunk. It's a given. The task is the comedy. A member of the audience could have been pulled on to the stage and asked to do the same thing with the same result. My head was not turned. Same thing with a guy playing a country wench. Seems I was inherently funny doing inherently funny things. What a surprise. 141 But this "lacking vocal interest" business...

Up to that moment, up until the moment I read that phrase, I had absolutely no conception of what it might be like for an actor to have "vocal interest." This is how dim and unreflective I was when it came to the nature of what I was doing. The implication that someone in the audience might be affected by my voice, might be enjoying my voice, might be taking a particular interest in my voice...Let me stop an unfurling sentence that has no foreseeable predicate on the horizon and confess that when I first began writing it, I put down "affected by your voice" and "enjoying your voice" and "particular interest in your voice." My first impulse was to dis-own the voice, to cast it on to an other. Even now in writing I am reluctant to claim it. You have to be made aware of the truth of the voice. You have to be initiated. You have to accept that it produces sensations that pass from you to the other. After all, what is at issue in psychosis? Who's voice is it? The voice is in you in ways beyond issues of ownership. It exists as a turn between you and not-you, between out and in, traversing space, closing distances. Even if you cover your ears, you feel the vibrations. It's a bit embarrassing. You have to get comfortable, which is not easy, and only then you can begin to have some distance and regard it as an object. You can play around with it. To say that I have since developed a vocal interest is to indulge in understatement, and it began with a word from an other.

IV

A number of years ago, our parish priest first asked me to organize the reading of the Passion for the Palm Sunday and Good Friday services. He liked the way I read when serving as lector and had gotten wind of my "theatre background." He was hoping for some kind of multi-player performance event. I did not want to do it. It was not in my nature to recruit the willing and the less willing, to beg and plead, to make back-up plans for when folks didn't show, to hold rehearsals for which no one would have time, to weigh questions of miking and not-miking. On top of that, the assumption was that I would read Jesus. I did not want to do that and organize at the same time. I would try to foist that responsibility on others, but it never worked out. Additionally, what with our priest having arrived from the ivy-wrapped North Atlanta avenues of Emory and Decatur, I knew he would want something interesting, something with conceptual clout, something that would confirm and validate my "theatre background." There were just not enough microphones for interesting, however. Or, alternatively, how could you be interesting if you had to rely on microphones? I suffered my reluctances. Inevitably, however, each year I ultimately pulled something together with the willing, guided by an ambitious but O so subtle and disciplining concept, and also read Jesus. I would begin my dreading process around Christmas of the previous year.

Finally our parish acquired a Music Associate, an actual staff person, also with a "theatre background," who now could organize the reading to fulfill a part of her job description.

I still had to read Jesus, however, but now free from administrative concerns, I had time to reflect. That means obsess. I had time to obsess. I became preoccupied with whether or not I was to act the role of Jesus as I read my text. I struggled with this every year, but this year my obsessing was more acute. What was my responsibility? Usually in a reading of scripture, one presents the text. I see it as my responsibility to provide text and space for contemplation. I try to set aside impulses to take up an imaginary relationship with the text and portray a speaker who might be a character other than myself. With the Passion reading it was feeling a bit different. The were multiple speakers, multiple roles, and even staging. There I was standing at the top of the steps in front of the altar, the center, the focal point. The Vanishing Point, all lines of intent and concern leading to the place where I stood. The Horizon of Meaning. Obsess, remember. I had time to obsess.

I was tempted and terrified at the same time as I entertained the possibility that at that moment I was truly called to channel the ghost of Antonin Artaud. Finally, there, then, at that place in time and space, what with the curtain of the temple coming down and the Alpha and the Omega impossibly coinciding for a preternatural instant, it was actually appropriate to regard myself as burning at the stake and signaling through the flames. After all, there is even a cry in another tongue: *Eli, Eli, lemma sabachthani!* And, yet, I could not resolve the issue to my satisfaction. I could cry out. I could be Jesus. I could cry out but not really. I could not so much cry as lift. I could not cry out at all but try, rather, to emphasize the otherness of the moment by pointing up the exotic glottal fireworks exploding in *sabachthani*. I put myself in the congregation. I sat in a pew and beheld myself up there. What was my responsibility? What was my role? How do I play this?

Could I solve the problem by trying to formulate a super-objective? I wondered if basic actor analysis could save me, could allow me to at least get my words out in a reasonable way. What did I want to do up there? What did I want to accomplish with my various utterances to Judas, Peter, disciples, Pilate, God, my fellow performers, the congregation, our priest?

I found my answer while praying to my Father in the Garden of Gethsemane. At that moment (we were running through the reading the day before) I uttered these words: *My Father, if it is possible, let this cup pass from me; yet not what I want but what you want.* Before and beyond and beneath any question of intent or objective was the actual truth of my performance: I was doing something I didn't really want to do. Of course! That is what I was offering in my performance. Up to that moment, I had been blind to the truth that was too close, too much woven in and around my being in the instant. I couldn't *see* it because I *was* it. I was up there because I had been asked to be up there and there was really nothing I could do about it. I didn't want to be there. I could certainly wish it was not the case, but... there I was. My misery, my dread, my obsessing, my confusion, my dissatisfaction, my doubts--there was no resolution. It was my performance. I was Jesus, *a man doing things he wished he didn't have to do.* No escaping it.

I, II, III & IV

Actors, dig in and work on that super-objective. It is your first and best defense against the other things that go on out of your awareness and control. Do what you can.

Each numbered lesson addressed the other things going on. Psychoanalysis calls them drives. When you attempt to explain them, you inevitably begin to sound like you are beginning a bedtime story: *a long time ago, before you were you, you were a pact with the other, an understanding, you communed and communicated via a system of paths and circulations and objects established in, on, and around your living body.* Upon this system of exchanges is built the complex self.

Language and learning take shape. Identity coalesces. Upon the drives is built the you who is the analyzing actor. But at the limits of your analysis, of your self, is the invisible realm of the drives continuing on. You will not be consulted now or in the future. You will not know. You can speculate and explore and hypothesize, but that is as clear as it will ever get. You can think of this kind of speculation as an optional supplement to questions of actions and objectives.

There are debates among the various camps about drives, but a few aspects seem fundamental and definitive. A drive has an object. A drive moves around the object. Movement is

144 endless. Beyond this, different theories take over and attempt different things. I embrace the Lacanian view because it emphasizes the permanence of the drives and the non-hierarchical, non-developmental nature of the drives. You don't achieve new drives as you mature. It's all there all the time, and there's no consistency or permanent coordination. This suits me. I also like the drives Lacan added to the classic line-up. In addition to the traditional Freudian oral and anal drives, we have have the invocatory and the scopic. Voice and vision. Both elemental in performance issues, I think. (No sexual drives? For Lacan such things take shape well within language, logic, and discourse, emerging as the speaking subject takes the stage and are, therefore, conceived and handled differently.)

Each lesson covers the invisible work of a drive. The object in each lesson serves as a pivot and a point of linkage between you and the other, between knowledge and ignorance, between clarity and opacity, between lack and fullness. Are you the drive or the object? And who is the subject if you are the object? You never know for sure.

I: the *oral* drive. It's object: the *breast*. This one takes a particularly playful turn in that I play the role of the other. The actress is the performer who is not aware that the truth of her work lies in my possession of her breast. An impossibility: she cannot act my appetite, yet it's constitutive. Additionally, in her hunger for a word from me, the director, I am also the breast.

II: the *anal* drive. It's object: *excrement*. Everything hinges on the possession of the necklace. I do not know exactly why I need it, but I know it holds the power. What is treasured? What is excremental? What is kept? What is sacrificed? Note how I seemed to struggle to squeeze out a few short paragraphs with this one.

III: the *invocatory* drive. It's object: the *voice*. The voice, at first, is not in my possession. I was not even aware it was lacking. Like each drive object, the voice is enjoyed. Singing as you go about household chores is supposed to be therapeutic.

IV: the *scopic* drive. It's object: the *gaze*. It's the point of blindness, pure and simple. As such, it's inherently paradoxical. What do you want? You want access to what is there to be seen? But you, in seeing, are seen. You want that. From an impossible perspective. As if the impossible is just covered up by the visible.

The Real Thing

Here are some tips for using the Vocal Sequence to work on a conventional scene, but the result doesn't necessarily have to remain conventional. It's up to you.

You have to accept a simple idea. Every play in performance has a particular life and energy as an event, as a distinct physical activity which strives to communicate to an audience. We could call it performance style. Throughout history and across cultures, performing artists have cultivated a variety of methods for creating meaningful physical events, acts of communication which use the laws of physics to achieve success. A poet of the theatre or a playwright is expecting such basic physics to serve the message–to, in part, be the message, or he or she would choose another medium. An actor, prior to any considerations of character or motive or message, is someone who is going to connect with an audience by harnessing the laws of physics. Sound and motion must pre-exist any notion of "inner truth." Sound and motion are your "inner-inner truth." Physical decisions are creative decisions. Actors cannot lose touch with physics as they negotiate the metaphysics of "the Method."

146

Actors move physical realities from the meaning-less to the meaning-full, informed by a desire to send a message. The problem is the transition from one state to another. As human beings we try to get to meaning as quickly as possible; as actors we shouldn't be afraid to take our time. You can use the Vocal Sequence to slow the transition process down. We are observing not only the world around us but also the raw, meaningless intensities within us; to develop a technique, a style, a mode of communicating our discoveries, will involve a coordination of both kinds of observation. Artists choose to dwell in non-meaning in an effort to formulate laws of creation. We continually run the risk with this kind of talk of getting too profound.

The Vocal Sequence is the same whether it's a play, a warm up, or some other creative fit. What is particular is how you time its use in your preparation for a role. You can work alone or with others. Accept that you are going to encounter raw physical truths first, a reason why it is good to work with actual lines within an actual scene, with something you will play on stage eventually.

Begin Vocal Sequence work with the material. This is the raw encounter. What are the elements: text, body/voice, other bodies/voices (perhaps), watchers (maybe), a physical space, objects (if you so choose)? Fundamental human physics without meaningful dress is always the first expectation. In the back of your mind you may be searching for particular things: a sound or body for the character, a certain playing rhythm, a dance of encounter with words or fellow actors, the seeds of a style, the "unconscious truth" of an event. But don't let your expectations close off the truth of the particular. Be prepared to be surprised and outraged.

Once a raw encounter is underway, a time for understanding begins. Remember that meaning tends to be phantasmagorical first before it gets grounded in laws and limits. Let it be extreme and phantasmagorical. Something about the body? A certain give and take? An unexpected welling up of emotion? A thought about the other? Your attitude at this point is uncertain: "I am not sure what is happening, but I have my suspicions…" You are testing the waters; assuming the worst. You may play out something which will never again see the light of day. Welcome discontinuities. Continuity is the dramatist's job. You can always return to the sequence and do something completely different. Ordering of events may begin to follow a dream logic. A circular logic. A spasmodic logic. You may tap into a vein of psycho-acoustic power and hit a stream which floods your entire approach to playing the part or the scene. You may see something. You may acquire some private knowledge. Making memories. "Good times…yeah, good times…"

Time to conclude should involve all participants, watchers and performers. You are in the basement of the Museum of Natural History surrounded by the specimens and artifacts you have collected on your expedition. You need to label a find before you can decide whether to store or display. Use the "world of the play" to help label. You need to decide which items you want to make available to all involved and which you want to keep to yourself. And you will find that labeling sometimes reduces the power of the discovery, you may choose to keep that one to yourself with a special label which only makes sense to you. What discovery can be displayed as "style?" As "performance techniques?" As "action and objective?" As "sense memory?" As "character biography?" As "blocking?" There's nothing like using Vocal Sequence work to get rid of those annoying "performance edition" blocking notes in the script. What about under the category "what the scene is really about?" Try some straight rehearsing of the material in light of the new knowledge. Give it time. Not every discovery will inform the scene. You may be surprised by how discoveries become part of the physical reality of your performance…later.

Here is a bit of a scene written by Hungarian playwright Ferenc Molnar:

(A scene from Molnar)

Don't be too quick to dismiss this as a corny love scene in a stiff English translation. Molnar's art is to show people trying to get bearings and steer a course on a ship being blown and tossed by love, all the while maintaining a certain sense of pretense and decorum. The "corny-ness" of it in the reading points us towards acknowledging it as requiring a certain elevation, a heightening, in the playing. The stakes are high, the feelings are real, the words demand a theatricalized lift to achieve an impact. Use the Vocal Sequence to make playing decisions for this scene, for characterization, for background, actions, sub-text, music and rhythm, and the physicalization of a style. No need to know more about the play. The sub-texts are still shifting and elusive even if you know what is going on. Use your exploration to fill in what appears to be missing. Here's another Molnar scene, a bit lighter, with real stakes but more whimsical in tone (though the previous scene could take that turn):

148

(Another scene from Molnar)

Let the Vocal Sequence lead you to making decisions about where the people are and what they might be doing as they speak. Don't necessarily gravitate toward the familiar and comfortable and try to make an outfit, i.e. a characterization, which you might wear in your daily life. Press yourself towards some theatricalization of life using the Sequence. Don't be afraid to dress yourself in unusual or exotic robes. Truth can be served by artifice, and many theatre-goers expect that to be a dimension of their experience. Move the scene toward that kind of complex expression. Our Performance Group Potlatch welcomes your comments.

On the physical act of writing...

Don't get me started. One of the elements in the Vocal Sequence is the Ideograph. If we look at the history of writing and alphabets and language, we find that the ideographs preceded the letters–the mark or inscription defined a cluster of notions. And was the mark a way of cutting a precise channel in the body, a way of rendering a particular bodily feeling to ground the lived meaning? Germanic children learned the runes by adopting body postures. Consider the cross as an ideograph, or the priest's postures during Mass or what was the true heart of DelSarte.

In an otherwise forgettable production of Romeo and Juliet I watched recently at the Performing Arts Center, at the moment of accepting the future possibility of death in the unfolding of her plan, Juliet was in a cold single spot at the front of the stage; she extended her arms at her side, not in a full cross, more at 45 degrees than 90, palms facing the audience, her look directed slightly above the audience (I'm too lazy to look up the closing couplet of the speech). But it was chilling. It was beautiful. The production was full of a frenetic "playerly" energy for the most part, but at that moment ideograph and moment and word lined up perfectly, all play stopped and boom: there was the full event in a nutshell. No need to continue. The production, alas, did continue.

I put the mark down and I watch it cutting a channel in me. What better way to render what never was.

More with four

Four corners. Each corner a performer. One performer issues and articulates thoughts: possibly "the Poet." A language
source. Another performer is "the Voice." Focuses on use of the
voice as a captivator, a force, an aesthetic object and energetic
activator. The third performer is "a sight for sore eyes." This
performer uses body and presence to hold the audience's visual
attention, to capture with presence. The fourth is a "Receiver"—representing an Audience impulse. This performer experiences all elements and attempts to reflect those vibrations
back into the chamber, but without recourse to "art." The "art"
is applied by the other three. All performers exert mutual influence upon one another as echoes in the chamber. Performers
also function as a series of stages or amplifiers or filters or processes through which "material" circulates.

Lacan's *Objet Petit (a)*

I am throwing Logan his Frisbee as usual. I sail the disk over a wide strip of ground in the backyard and he makes the snatch with sublime acrobatic grace. It is a transcendent process, a few formulas from the mathematics of nature writ down in a series of perfect acts.

Ike is feeling better now that he's on pain medication. He has the energy this morning to descend the stairs from the porch into the backyard and sniff out a place to perch and poop. I stop throwing for a moment to watch. We have been encouraged to monitor his pooping. A soft pudding is extruded. Not great, but no spewing. It holds its shape and coils into a neat pile that glows brownish-green in the morning sunshine. Ike serenely moves on in search of tasty weeds to chew.

The process of Frisbee throwing is now complicated. Logan will run anywhere to make his catch. He certainly wouldn't put on the brakes to avoid stepping in a pile of Ike's poop. I don't want him stepping into it and trailing residue all over the porch, so I have to throw to an area of the backyard where he will not run that risk. Every time I prepare to throw, I locate the pile, its color making it easy to see in the yard, and I launch the disk. I have to factor in the pile before each throw. The pile controls certain aspects of this activity that were free and open-ended (from my point of view) before. One could even say that the pile is now the only real thing in view and that I ignore it at my peril.

151

Such is the place of the (a) in the subject's unconscious. It is the thing around which all movement is negotiated and orchestrated. It, once lodged into place, is never not taken into account. It's effect as a noxious bodily remainder is significant. An actual encounter with it would be unacceptable, but its existence is influential and holds a place perpetually in perceptions and the shaping of intentions.

This is very basic stuff. Carry on.

Now I want my poetry to do what I should have been doing all along with photo albums, home movies, and journal notebooks. It's kind of pathetic, really.

All this debate over whether or not sex is religious. It always ends with someone asking for forgiveness, doesn't it?

Artists my age are supposed to be eating their own livers with a malevolent gusto, but I still don't have the stomach for it.

152 I think I'm some kind of compromise between Sisyphus and Priapus. Trying to roll my rock and perpetually hurting myself.

Why my waxing and waning: same old manifesto

Two supply priests exhibited the elements that interest me. One possessed a deeply resonant voice which he employed in a wonderfully archaic homiletic style. He was in his seventies so maybe not so archaic for him. You could imagine a Nineteenth-Century American declamatory style of oration (and acting) at it's best. But most effective was the way he linked his manner with his rhetoric. Use of ellipsis. Use of *non sequitur*. Use of wit. Effortlessly conjuring a theatre of mind and heart. The other was an African American man in his sixties. His style was not really what I associate with classic Black Gospel/ Pentecostal style. More of what I would characterize as a classic, spiritually large African American "thespian" or histrionic (in the best sense of the word) approach. He stood in front of the altar, unanchored to ambo. His voice occupied a plaintive register, as if his voice was the sole representative of the human condition in its pain and longing for transcendence. Somewhat improvisational, but not built on repetitions as much as on waves of intensity. He very much evoked for me Grotowski's notion of the actor as sacrificial agent with his address to us as also an impersonation of our collective sense of soul.

153

Yes, the rhetorical moves can be composed, documented, recreated. I'm more intrigued by what we might separate out as essential but unscriptable: aspects of voice and physical engagement, non-verbal energies of impersonation.

I have great admiration for Neo-Futurism (our current focus and project) as an attempt to precipitate the most compelling and effective aspects of what I would call a Theatre of Wit. It's a conceptual compositional challenge. I can pretend to be clever if I set the scene properly, but my interests really lie elsewhere. Cleverness and wit of conception are not capacities I can use consistently to "make theatre." It's a put on, for me, a struggle to keep up, a frustrating deficit. So I wax and wane. Theatre guy but not a "theatre guy." It's not a paradox I enjoy, I assure you!

So I want to reaffirm my interests, primarily for myself. It's easy to lose touch with them. As a potential performer, my goals and interests produce a great deal of fear and dread in me as I think about trying to bring such things to the table. I thought it might make more sense to collaborators if I tried to list these things, so you might understand my fears and see how you respond. Maybe what I fear is bread and butter for you. If so, I crave your input and guidance.

- Not only must I be ready to bear witness to everything, but I must be ready to encounter everything.

- I want to isolate, identify, contemplate, and celebrate every little moment, behavior, atmosphere, sounds, image, gesture, pause, accident, and notion. I wish to ponder those. I wish to compose with those.

- There has to be a perverse push to intimacy in my actions. I must assume the same urge in everyone.

- I want to try to converse using non-verbal, non-rational, embodied elements. I want these conversations to be both banal and sublime. I want to be happy when something goes nowhere.

154

- I want to explore what these difficult and elusive components of a performing body trigger. I look for elusive terrain.

- I am more interested in the audience's response to events than in telling stories. I'm not good at telling stories, so I'm always searching for something for which I have a working facility.

- I'm always trying to traumatize myself with the unprecedented.

But here's the thing. I don't want this to be interpreted as my declaration of a desire to scandalize or shock. It would be easy to exploit this manifesto for assorted personal agendas. That's part of my fear and dread. Eliciting whispers and tittering is no fun for me. I guess I want the "push to intimacy" to be somewhat heroically philosophical and omnipresent, a give and take that flows as naturally as water. It may be an impossible ideal because it's not something I can assume readily. I've witnessed performers/researchers assume it, but I mostly stood cut-off and uncertain about my role. It's a difficult thing to ask of people. I fear asking it of myself. I've seen it and I've witnessed the conversations unfold (many years ago), but re-creating the climate and including myself as a motivating agent is difficult.

The supply priests encouraged me not to worry if my interests are solely rooted in memory and past traumas. These performance possibilities are part of our lives and experiences now. It's reassuring to be reminded of that. These elements are viable and vital. I will continue to ponder them.

What I have not done with this manifesto is draw far reaching conclusions for the kinds of work that might begin. I need to think about that. I invite others to do so.

Sure, therapy is fun, until somebody loses an I.

At Wit's End...A-W-E....

We want our own Wits Untied.

Two woots or two to woot? Which?

Marketers. They know me and call me by name.

The terrifying reality of absolute freedom. A plunge into depthless and abyssal possibility. The true and primal anxiety of choice..Facing that final existential limit. Just as long as I'm back from the store with bay leaf by five.

Go carefully, Facebook friends. The air gets very thin once you reach the higher platitudes.

I seem original only because I pull from a broader assort- ment of clichés.

Enigma Alignment: a *theory and practice for creating performances leaning upon a psychoanalytic understanding of the human condition*

The Oxford Dictionary of Current English is a thick but practical paperback and does not linger over etymology or historical moments of emergence and usage. Lucky you. It merely states that an enigma is a "mysterious or puzzling person or thing." It does add one etymological tidbit in this case: from the Greek word for *riddle*.

157

To gain a psychoanalytic understanding of the person and why he or she creates art, you have to imagine a doughnut. A doughnut is an object with a hole. You could say a doughnut exists to illustrate what a hole is, since without the doughnut you would have no hole. And without the hole, you'd have no doughnut. The existence of the doughnut depends on the existence of the hole. It depends on the lack of a center. It depends on nothing. Or it depends on something, but that something is missing.

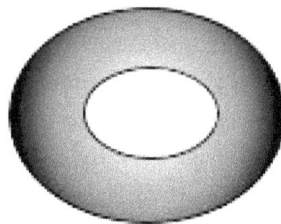

One could argue a doughnut is what it is and is not missing anything. The hole, the missing center, is just a projection on our part. We attribute a hole because we are comparing the doughnut to something else, to a baseball or a cube, for instance, both of which are "whole" objects with nothing "lacking." Couldn't the doughnut also be considered whole, w(ithout)hole? Sure. We can choose to see it as an object like any other object, lacking nothing. We can think that. Just as we can think it with a hole. We can think either thing. Imagination is a great asset and allows us to dream a dream of wholeness for the doughnut. After all, why exclude the doughnut from the whole thing club? Why see through the eyes of petty prejudice? But at the level of structure, a doughnut is a torus, which in the mathematics of topology (surfaces) means, sidestepping the math, you cannot traverse its surface in the same way you might traverse a ping pong ball or a box or a can of fruit cocktail. Visualize it: you can sort of imagine being an ant and setting out upon a journey on a basketball, knowing if you stay the course on a certain line of travel, you will wind up back where you began. Any "whole" object will guarantee such a direct and complete journey. With the doughnut, however, if your ultimate goal is to return to the starting place, the hole is always going to complicate the journey. To have a straight, unswerving journey you would have to avoid the hole entirely and set a course around the outer rim, trying to act as if the object were not a doughnut. So, for our purposes, let's contend with the hole as a real thing, a structural presence (or absence), something which complicates the game.

158

The initial psychoanalytic wager involves seeing the person as a doughnut, as a thing which lacks something. And the lacking makes living somewhat complicated as well as somewhat interesting, to understate the situation…somewhat. To read more deeply into the whys and wherefores of this lack would take us into psychoanalytic writers like Freud, Jung, Lacan, and others. For our purposes, let's jump the student immersion stage, assume we've done the reading, undergone our own analysis, even, and move to the implications for artist and audience.

How does an artist contend with the hole in the doughnut? In an initial flood of comprehension you might assert: *Fill the hole with the work of art!* And the short response to that is: *Yes!* But the artist has spent some time contemplating his or her own hole and knows nothing is quite that simple. But thinking this way has given us two provisional parts of a structure. The artist wants to fill the hole in the doughnut, yes, but whose hole? The artist has a hole which the process of creating and the object created try to fill…somewhat. And the audience for the artist's work is attempting to fill a hole through the encounter with the work. You, as an appreciator, as an audience, are bringing the object to the place of your lacking,

your hole. Artist and Audience. Two doughnuts, two holes. Is that it?

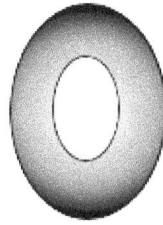 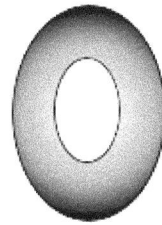

Artist   Audience

Clearly we are being led to something else. After all, another psychoanalytic wager involves saying two is…somewhat insufficient for a complete structure. With art making we must include the work of art itself. The *third* thing, then, we might assert, is the object. For the sake of making a structure, let's continue to see the artist and audience 159 as doughnuts and add the third object, the art object. Is the art object serving to fill two holes in two doughnuts? Or is the object something else? Perhaps the object is also a donut, serving as a reflection or a semblance or a likeness of the other two. Is there an effort to fill the holes with a third donut?

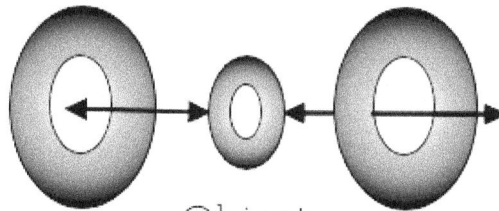

Object

Let's try to make this all a bit more meaningful as far as the work of the artist goes. Let us assume we are performing artists who might work in the realm of the drama or might not. We may or may not be engaged in telling a story, but we are without doubt engaged in producing a performed event for an audience. We do, without doubt, occupy a dimension of meaning in our performing. Even if we set out only to produce sensations which frustrate sense, we have to use the dimension of meaning to establish some kind of connection with the audience, a basic contract if nothing else. Now think about this hole in the doughnut. Think about the ways this hole is experienced by a human being. Think about how an experience of a hole can be communicated. In the realm of meaning, what is the most fundamental way such a lack can be represented? What is this hole? How is it experienced? Why is it there? Where does it lead? When does it appear? What? Why? How? Where? When? ? ? ? Another wager of psychoanalysis (and of many expressions of dramatic theory, too, by the way) is that the *question* is the fundamental symbolic structure for expressing our constitutional lack, that inside the hole in the doughnut is a question mark. The artist, then, in contemplating the hole in the doughnut, is contemplating a question. The performing artist, when engaged in working with the hole, with somehow filling it through an act, is engaged with a question. Every creative act is rooted in a question. If this is true, then every created object is built upon a question. And if this is true, then every art object, every performance in our case, can be seen as having a question at its constituted center. Voila! Now we have

160 three doughnuts. Three holes. Three questions. Our art of performance works with these three donuts, whether we are engaged in dramatic storytelling, improvisation, temporal image making, musical expression, playing games, or anything which involves an audience, an artist, and creating an object (or event or story or...).

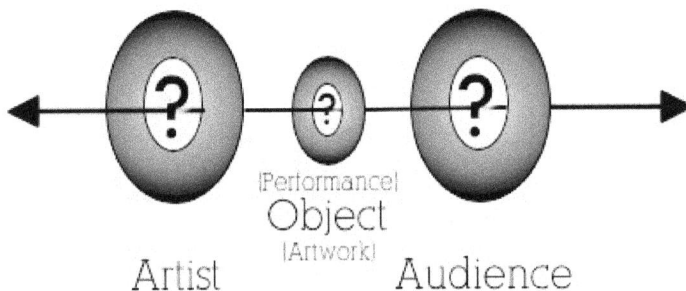

Artist — [Performance] Object [Artwork] — Audience

Already we have a very complex structure, but it can be complicated even further.

Our three doughnuts are brought together through convention, custom and culture–three forces which create, protect and guarantee our basic opportunity to attempt art for an audience. Think of these forces as shaping a privileged arena in which we are able to ask our questions. We have to acknowledge a fourth thing which assures meaning for our three doughnut questions. Think of it in a wider sense as the very words and ideas we use to ask our questions. Think of it as the place where an audience can meet us halfway and gain some understanding. We are given meaning and structure through it, our names and family networks being two concrete examples. We are led to understand ourselves as doughnuts because of it. We experience the possible and the impossible because of it. We exist in it knowing our questions will not always get answered. Let's call it…not another doughnut, even though it can seem like a doughnut at times, with its own set of human qualities and lacks. Let's just call it a *place*, with the existence of artists and audience and objects holding a position in its midst. And it does have holes, this place, because the artists, the audiences and the objects have holes; we are a part of the place and we have holes, and the holes seem to go all the way through. But we cannot call it a doughnut with 100 percent certainty since we are uncertain if it is being seen from a sufficient distance by someone or something with the ability to identify doughnuts. There's a question there. A hole in our knowledge.

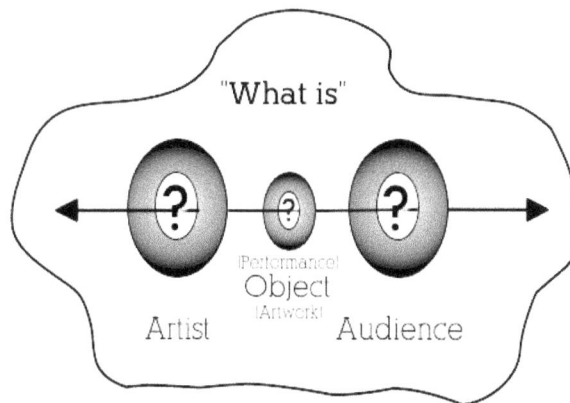

So we have established some kind of outer boundary for our structure, where we confront a question and are taken back to our hole, our lack, our own question. And so let's ask how our little model can help us as artists as we contemplate the question and create new work. It's important to understand this question in the center of the doughnut as a fundamental question, as an intimate question. Not necessarily something you would readily chat about at a party. And it helps to know that for the audience, the same intimate interior is at stake.

The artist must bring an inner experience of the question into alignment with the audience's experience of its own intimate interior (and the audience is really a collection of individuals, each with an intimate interior, mass effects arise from various co-ordinations of the truths we have in common). Intimate questions touch upon desires, needs, wishes, fears, fantasies, dreams, death, God, the future, evil, non-existence, the past, the body, love, appetite, obsession, enjoyment, and fulfillment. You get the idea. And keep in mind that the contemplation of the intimate interior can produce a variety of responses from the sublime and sorrowful to the giddy and ridiculous (in case you think that our model is insisting a performer's art has to be perpetually serious and profound). The object, then, can be seen as a way to frame the possibility of asking the intimate question or of experiencing the intimate interior. Or the object could represent the intimate question. It could stage the question, amplify the question, modify the question. The object might be offered as an answer. It might attempt to stage an answer. And most audaciously, the object could fill the hole and bring an end to lack. *Bah-dah-bing.* Certainly more than one performer has presumed to attempt as much. The most dangerous of games. Why not try? An intimate question to be sure.

162 *Two proposals based on the above:*

The artist brings an audience through time (performance art involves time) to the intimate interior, to the question, to dwell there in a manner of the artist's choosing.

Alternatively, the artist produces an event out of the intimate interior which affects an audience's intimate interior.

These are just two propositions. You can use the doughnut model to make any number of proposals about art. Think of one which will take you somewhere.

Contemplate the model with the idea of the object as a performance. Try drawing provocative conclusions. For example, you could see the audience and artist doughnuts as being in a mirror relation, with the mirror plane resting at the place of the object. Hold, as 'twere, a mirror up to nature...Hamlet's advice to the players. We see how a performance event can involve a mimesis of some kind. Or we can imagine artist and audience both looking into a mirror and gasping, "That's me!" The act of identification is possible. The mirror captivates. Or consider the alienation of the image in the mirror: "That's me, but it's not me, and it's not how others really see me; it's reversed." For Alice the mirror was a portal to some other place, familiar and unfamiliar. Or think about what it means to capture a reflection of a question. Or think about the object as transparent, then as reflective, then as some kind of blot which gets in the way. Any thought can lead to a strategy for developing a performance event. Any thought can be brought to bear on an intimate question.

A performance event is a temporal event. Time passes. Something is moving. Can we see the possibility of movement in our model? We can see our doughnuts change over time if we wish. Perhaps the holes get larger. Perhaps the doughnuts take shape over time. Do we see the object take shape as a doughnut or as the filling for a hole. Is the hole in the doughnut disguised? We can see something transmitted among the three doughnuts over time. What is transmitted? Something shaping the rim of the interior. The intimate question. An intimate transmission. What circulates? How? Something involving the eyes, the ears. Voices. Bodies. Movement. Meaning. There's something very private and non-negotiable about what transpires at the place of the question. Some bodily truths are absolute. Seeing and hearing, sounding and showing, all of the fundamental elements which carry messages, questions and answers, emerging through the agency of the body, taking up residence in the place where something lacks. Meanings, too, fulfill and frustrate, traveling the perimeter of the question. To think it in this way is to see the work of art as a system of relays. This is just one way to think it, of course.

Perhaps you want to focus on the wide, embracing fourth realm. Think about how this place of encyclopedic abundance gives shape to our intimate questions. What is the world and who are we? Here, of course, is the terrain of the great playwrights, of our storytellers. Every conceivable situation is granted possibility through the agency of the fourth thing. It's somewhat inescapable. As artist, how do you want your alignment of mysteries, artist, object, audience, to sit with respect to what is? What about this world you, the artist, are creating? What conventions will you adopt or overturn? What social dictates will you knot into the event and toward what end? What great strands tangle in such a way as to produce your intimate question? And the actor is perhaps a masterful tangler and un-tangler of knots? Or think of the actor, perhaps, as someone who can focus very specifically on what it is to exist with respect to this widest realm and who uses the three doughnut orientation to decide upon what to do in the world of the story. To quote Dr. Seuss: "O the things you can think…"

Things to make and do. Use our enigma alignment model to create some simple improvisation games or a scheme for writing. For instance:

- The intimate question will remain unspoken.
- Try answering a question through simple symbols and bodily expression.
- What does the other wish me to do? Who does the other wish me to be?
- Create a point of obscurity.
- Make a place where the answer to the question is Death.
- Elaborate and enjoy a private joke.
- Tantalize, provoke and withhold.
- Use a translating medium. Success or failure. Warmer, colder.
- What is lacking? Try to respond.

164

He still will at less
than a moment's
notice strip down
to his Lyotard and...
dance, dance, dance.

He cannot help himself.

Exceptionalism for Dummies

Trying to invent a form of solitaire in which you have to mislead your opponent.

What's really going on with vampires: born out of anxieties related to concerns for bloodlines and kinship and fears about intertribal marriage. The legends possibly began emerging as the bourgeoisie started to assume these formerly aristocratic concerns through their more immediate and familiar fears of "foreigners" and other such threats. Thoughts? Observations?

Politeness

We've been watching the original *Dark Shadows* on Netflix Instant View. (No, we're not hip enough to have known that Depp and Burton were doing a remake. Found that out later as I looked for links. It was truly just a desire to relive childhood memories.) As the vampire Barnabas Collins made his entrance into the action over ten or so twenty-minute segments, I became quite preoccupied with his politeness. Something about the totality of it–its comprehensiveness. Obviously, he wants to be accepted into the family at Collinswood and not arouse suspicion. It pays for him to be on his best behavior. Soon enough he will be making some pretty significant requests of folks, so it's not to his advantage to upset anyone. Charm is his skeleton key. But there's more to it, I think. The character Maggie, already under a certain amount of hypnotic influence, notes how his "old world" manners seem linked to a profound sense of loneliness and isolation. What she doesn't know this early on, of course, is the true nature of this separateness and the true depth of it.

I am struck by how this simple soap managed to create something dark and palpable through such rudimentary and minimal means. I found myself nodding along with Barnabas as he spoke in various scenes to various characters he wished to charm and influence. I, too, was appreciating what was at stake as he reached out from a position of absolute separateness. I was in the game, and there was not one special effect to lure me along through its magic. Barnabas is nothing but what he can say, and he gets nothing except through what he can say, so he must say it in a very precise way. The script at times even has him discriminating properly between the uses of who and whom. What we are witnessing is Vampire Minimalism crafted wholly through language. Sure, soon enough there will be teeth and biting and fluids, and we know something is afoot behind the veneer, but the essence of the vampire is in the words. As if seizing upon a spoken politeness that is palpably archaic, or dead, he extends a powerful reach into the world of the living with its unsuspecting casualness and neglect and its trivial cares. His banishment from us and his appetite for us are expressed in his strange, antique precision.

Another Tom Jones

From a procrastinate Tom Jones, Book II, Chapter 2:

"To deny that beauty is an agreeable object to the eye, and even worthy of some admiration, would be false and foolish. Is not Love like candy on a shelf? You want to taste and help yourself, do you not?" The Reverend began to warm to his theme, particularly as the question of Mrs. Quiver's recent escapades required extensive commentary and earnest moral reflection. *"Mind you, it's not unusual to be loved by anyone. Nor is it not unusual to have fun with anyone."*

Let us briefly at this moment, dear reader, note how the Reverend was in no way oblivious to the true factitious presence of the lady in question. Her breathing--dare we go further and suspect panting--presence was tempting the periphery of his homiletic sights even as he nudged his arguments toward the politely non-disputable. "It's not unusual to be mad with anyone. It's not unusual to be sad with anyone."

"And yet." Mr. Norbutwait could not resist the opportunity for interjection. "She's the kind I'd like to flaunt and take to dinner." In his urgency he seemed most unaware that his punctuation of the Reverend's disquisition had become a confession. He became transformed. "And she always knows her place. She's got style. She's got grace. She's a winner."

Alas, poor Norbutwait at this moment was a plaything of his humours. Mrs. Quiver's eyes, however, betrayed nothing, and the Reverend's extemporizing was not to be eclipsed by such fevered tender display. "We're always told repeatedly, the very best in life is free and if you want to prove it's true, baby I'm telling you, this is what you should do."

The Reverend seemed to reverse course at this moment, and are you not, patient reader, wholly relieved. "These matters are of a very delicate nature, and the scruples of modesty should compel us, nay command us, even with our knowing it is never modesty's place to command."

We may discern the Reverend's precipitous halt is noted by Mrs. Quiver, whose eyes catch the shuffling churchman's at this point. It takes but the lady's mouthing of a certain intimacy, "What's new, Pussycat," to Mr. Norbutwait's surmise, to bring the Reverend toppling into an impromptu translation a certain passage from one of Horace's lesser regarded eclogues:

Just help yourself to my lips

To my arms just say the word, and they are yours

Just help yourself to the love,

In my heart your smile has opened up the door.

"O, dear lady, I long simply to touch the green, green grass of home." The Reverend, falling upon his knees with this expostulation, gathered a portion of Mrs. Quiver's skirt in his hands and began mopping his brow.

"But to make this the sole consideration of marriage," said Lady Quiver, laying a hand upon the shoulders of the dear Reverend, shoulders that continued to lurch in tearful confession, "to lust after it so violently as to overlook all imperfections for its sake, or to require it so absolutely as to reject and disdain religion, virtue, and sense, which are qualities in their nature of much higher perfection, only because an elegance of person is wanting: this is surely inconsistent, either with a wise man or a good Christian. And this point I must come to Mr. Norbutwait's defense. He always runs while others walk. He acts while other men just talk. He looks at this world, and wants it all."

Mr. Norbutwait did not hesitate to take an opportunity so generously offered. "So I strike, like Thunderball."

"O why, why, why Delilah," was what the Reverend muttered as he rose to his feet.

Stuck in his thumb
and pulled out a plum
and said, "What a good boy am I!."
  --the essence of all intellectual ambition.

'

Assert your absolute.
I don't give a hoot.

Now working exclusively with found objections.

Reality has been altered in imperceptible ways.

Was going to write a status post about clowns and age, but it was too many characters. Seriously. No word play here. Just a report on the state of things.

Notes the word "rapacious" is spot on and powerful whenever he uses it, but embarrassing and pretentious when used by some flavor-of-the-month artist/intellectual in an NPR interview. Baffling.

Maybe all of the "blood of patriots" people and all of the "blood of martyrs" people could sit in the same tub and enjoy a "blood bath."

To exploit the system from below is to be a bum; to exploit the system from above is to be a competitor; to accept the system as it is is to be a fool. Is that about right?

I'm mature enough now to know my lack of brains is not due to lack of brains.

Postmodern Theatre in a nutshell:
Antigone sports a berkka
while Kanye leads a masurka.

From their nests
all are pests
take your pick
a flea, a tick
you scratch, you're sick
none are neat-o
damn mosquito!

Suddenly struck by the phrase "wiggle room."

Farce

I'm opening a space in which I want us to think about Farce. Part of this is my attempt to pick brains as I prepare for this summer. I want to offer something to the GHP Theatre minors called Farce Factory, an opportunity to write and produce short (and why not as short as five minutes) farces. My wager is that the students will have an appreciation of farce as a structure, and will "know it when they see it," but they will lack an understanding of how difficult it is to construct. I could, in fact, propose that the ability to construct farce is on its way out as an imaginative capacity. If this is true, can it be resurrected? Or am I just going through the middle-aged pining for some non-existent golden age? Am I just focusing on my own *agalma* by recognizing something in my own appreciation for farce?

At any rate, the students and I will take a look at some examples of farce form and try to be very Aristotelian in identifying the defining elements. So suggest some examples, please. Feydeau's plays (including speculation of why the revival of *Hotel Paradiso* had its own ring in the Inferno,–and how was *Lend Me a Tenor ?*), *Fawlty Towers*, and the plot mechanisms of *The Court Jester* (the whole story arc is more comedic than farcical, I think, but the specific situations played out are farce)–these are some obvious examples. What I'm hoping is that we can isolate enough traits to create our own handbook on farce construction. If you have your own ideas about necessary strategies, let me know. I'll throw out a principle to get the discussion going. Farce requires what I call "the eyes of the Law." Anyone want to take up that provocative assertion? Also, is farce less tolerated (and more difficult to consciously fabricate at a high level of complexity) in a culture of increasing religious conservatism and concern for "traditional family values?" Farce, after all, acknowledges our divided nature as beings who both want the Good and want to get off. Such a view of the human predicament is, perhaps, too ambivalent to be tolerated in this current climate.

Catching up with comments…

Continue offering definitions. Part of the fun of the form game is to make an assertion, such as there is a form of drama called farce, and let the nature of the form take shape as people offer definitions. Do I have a definition? I, like anyone, have my notions.

I would agree that there is an element of the excessive that is crucial, not only in the situations depicted but also in the aspects of character portrayed. The Braggart Soldier is a farcical character. The Zealot, the Lecherous Old Man. Yes, I think *Seinfeld* operates in the world of farce not only through the way it cuts away to the "worst case scenario" (a type of exaggeration) with any notion, but also in the way it will isolate a trait in a character and generate the humor from the isolated trait in play (exaggeration of focus).

It's ironic that the playing out of an overblown situation and the presence of impossible complications can only happen through an attention to detail. I assert that farce is most dependent on a detailed knowledge of how things work, and I am not only referring to mechanical things but also to institutional things and social things (etiquette, custom, etc). Those aspects of our world that can be described in formulas are the richest for formulaic manipulation and complication. And the essence of farce is recognizing that the formulas are at work and in play in every aspect of our existence. They control us; autonomy is an illusion. And it is only in the presence of formulas that we can contend with the possibility of making mistakes, another crucial feature of farce.

I also agree with the notion of farce depicting a drive for satisfaction which exceeds all bounds of restraint. Feydeau and company were Freudians before Freud (or with Freud) and their plays were laboratory experiments using Civilization and its Discontents as subjects. But farce is not modern, per se, since the notion of appetite is timeless.

And there's another irony, the farce as art form requires a huge amount of differed gratification in the act of preparation. A complicated farce implies that an artist has thought deeply and analytically about the terrain and chased down the worst implications of the existing order of things. And the result has to be accurate, overwhelming, and remorseless. And there has to be at least one final twist more than you could envision in your worst nightmare.

Aha. Relationship between farce and horror. So the only decent farce I've seen in the past year or so may be *Saw*. It's all about what the writer does once the anxiety has been created. Does it have to resolve in laughter?

Beauty

When a farce is successful, you invariably hear comments about the beauty of its construction, about its meticulousness. And in the enjoyment of the farce, aren't we both inside with the anxiety of events while also outside contemplating the perfection of the abstract structure? It is this aspect of farce, this notion of plotting as sublime triumph, that compels me to think that the beauty of farce lies in the beauty of a mathematics. There is also the sense of a farce being a perfect clockwork physical system in action, but every physicist will tell you, it's nothing until you get the equations right.

Can we say that farce is a branch of mathematics? Could one, perhaps, do "farce" on any set of propositions no matter how abstract as long as certain terms and operations are brought into play? Ives' *All in the Timing* is, it seems to me, a farce made with certain propositions about time and the stuff of language. Beckett's "minimalist" scripts are instances of farce operations at work with severely circumscribed sets of material. Stoppard's preferred mode, child of Wittgenstein that he is, is farce since he, in his plays, is usually examining a set of propositions posited as truth. These propositions are subjected to farce operations.

Farce posits a *situation* (which implies a temporality, a necessary proposition for a farce operation to proceed?–a spacing, perhaps, not reducible to a symbol–a temporal frame, perhaps) and defines the situation with a number of propositions, equations, givens, the stuff of the initial situation set. What elements are essential to a farce operation? A *farce set*, perhaps, is a potential identity set. Some entity seeks to define itself with respect to the propositions of the set. But its a particular kind of identity, one that torments logic, perhaps–notA is A, or A is B. Here's the need for a temporality: in farce, an agent seeks identity by passing through the propositions of a set to a position of *A is Not the Set A*. Another name for Set A is *The Law*. The farcical agent seeks identity with *what is not The Law*, but can only achieve this by passing through The Law and actually scrambling its propositions within the temporal frame. Simple example: An agent, a, is to establish identity with set A (The Law) through a farce operation, f. A=(2+2=4), therefore you could say a = not (2+2=4). No farce, however, just identity by negation. And in theory, there is no temporal frame, t, because simple negation is instantaneous. A farce operation with agent a is a(f) =t[2+2(n)=4] where n is any damn thing and t[] defines the temporal frame. There are more than one answer to a(f) if A is given as (2+2=4), but there is not a set of infinite answers. Just a bunch. t[2+2=5] is a potential a(f) of a, as is t[2+2=onion]. a(f)=t[oops I spilled my coffee] is valid so long as set A [2+2=4] was active in the temporal frame,t[], at some point. In other words, we have to trust that the operation is being honest with us. So is this the farcical operation at its most abstract? Discuss.

Identity implies two things: desire for completion and the possibility of deception.

Farce operations explore, therefore, for some agent, all manner of relationships to identity within the temporal frame which involve manipulating the elements of a potential identity set. Farce theory, therefore, is concerned with describing all possible events within the temporal frame as the agent passes through The Law in the quest for identity. The propositions within the set, The Law, are both identity elements and obstacles to identity (necessary obstacles–the agent meets resistance from the elements in the very act of carrying out the farce operation).

There are only so many ways to scramble a number of given propositions within a temporal frame. It depends to a certain extent on the initial propositions in the set and the count of the temporal frame. Remember, the farce operation is not instantaneous, so its duration implies a count, a succession of moments within the temporal frame. How to best represent this symbolically is one of the great still unsolved challenges of farce theory. The blink is still our best bet.

The *blink* is the timing of the temporal frame. Let's return to our Set [2+2=4]. To place this set within a temporal frame, t[], and begin farce identity operations, here's what you do:

[2+2=4]

now, blink…

t[4+2=2]

you have accomplished the minimal farce operation on the set and have achieved a(f)…the rest is gravy…blink…

t[2+1=4]

now, blink…

t[2-2=4]

now, blink…

t[2-2-2-2=4]

and, blink…

t[slowly I turn step by step~#%$4]

and, blink…

t[two plus two equals four]

and, even, blink…

t[for team blequals plush]

to ultimately, blink…

t[like sands through the hourglass so are the days of our lives]

Discuss.

Okay, I got a little silly.

But, many of the notions I just toyed with do play their part in farce: an agent with desire or drive (not necessarily for "completion"–but why do we go after things?), the rules or governing principles of The Law (yes, not necessarily "The Law," more an absolute principle of "the way things are" and statements about what will happen if you try to subvert or ignore "the way things are"), a possibility of deception, a chance that things will not work according to expectation, a chance that things will work beyond expectation, obstacles, a sense of time being marked by twists and turns, and details of the established universe combining and working into a perverse arrangement. And a sense of it being a beautiful arrangement.

I come back to the idea of analysis. Only by knowing the full implications and workings and laws at work in a given universe can you fully realize the creation of subversions and problems in that universe. Feydeau: determine the two people who should not meet under any circumstances and then bring them together as quickly as possible. And usually this meeting is going to function as some kind of obstacle to someone attempting to get something greatly desired. And if the explosion unfolds beautifully (every i dotted and t crossed), so much the better.

So what are the implications for composing farce? And what are the implications for improvising farce?

Establish the Situation Set . And decide if the audience is privy to every element in the set at the outset. The full set only has to be revealed by the end.

Determine an agent who has a drive or desire possibly prohibited by the Laws at work in the Situation Set.

Determine which elements of the Situation Set to withhold from the agent.

Develop elements of the set as obstacles to the agent and implement those obstacles.

Does the agent enlist other agents to help obtain a desire?

A variation on this plan might be to envision an agent and a desire first, then construct a situation set which contains and prohibits the realization of that desire.

Can an agent's desire be modified to overcome the elements in the situation set? (I have a sneaking suspicion that overcoming through modification is closer to comedy than farce. Love allows for transformation.)

Part of the game in farce is distribution of knowledge. The complete Situation Set only exists without gaps and questions in the mind of some abstract entity; the audience occupies the position of that entity only in the last temporal blink. Till then, everyone, audience included, has incomplete knowledge. The irony for the agent is that it is the incompleteness of knowledge that makes desire possible (if you know everything, you know you can't win).

Everything must be deduced from the propositions in the Situation Set in a way that seems inevitable. That's part of the beauty. Everything comes about through what is given. The arbitrary can only operate if the Situation Set holds a place for the arbitrary.

177

Organic: it means those tiny little seeds are still in there.

Is it desire or *jouissance*? It depends on where you place the potted plant.

You want to power your political machine. There are two batteries: one is labelled "Reason," the other is labelled "Conviction." Which do you hook up to?

A noonday gimlet is no gimmick. It is real. It is true.

178

Hysterical Hygene-assist

This is something of a variation on a Meisner exercise (but not really; it's its own animal; closer to being on the couch). It is designed to bring you into contact with some aspect of the Other, to do and think and be yourself in the presence of this Other with no acting required. In fact, it is a way to practice shrugging off that nagging impulse to act. We might work with this some in class to refine the method, but it is primarily designed as something to do away from the work, when you are tired of making things up but want to create with someone outside of tedious soap-operatic options. It compels you as a person to entertain some new depths.

Sit with a partner, facing each other comfortably, close but not intimately so. One of you is to simply be yourself (a terrifying prospect for many actors). The other is to seem to be his or herself but will actually do something quite *unnatural*. There will be a cycle of actions and then the roles of being and seeming change.

The actor who is being his or herself begins to speak to the other actor. No acting. Just speak to this other person you know in a way which would be comfortable.

The other is in the seat of the Other. To sit in the place of the Other you should seem to be yourself but with some important differences. You do not answer questions. You do not try to meet demands. You listen and assure the speaker you are truly listening. But you must listen in a particular and somewhat unusual way. You listen to the speech with an ear toward hearing something other than what is being said (you are *the Other*, after all). Once you have heard something different, you give it back to the other person. What does it mean to hear something other than what is being said? By forgetting that you know a person is talking to you and listening just to the speech. What if you chopped off part of a sentence or phrase? What if you pulled out a word or a slip of speech? Would it imply some different meaning? What if you re-punctuated or searched for puns? What if you answered some question which was not asked? What if you simply emphasized a word? Or asked for a meaning to be made explicit? Homonyms or antonyms? You are scanning the speech waiting for something else to happen and then you deliver your discovery (no matter how irrelevant) to the speaker. And you shape your *intervention* in a particular way. You don't want to do a great deal of talking. Keep your response short and somewhat vague. Do not offer any explanation for how or why you formulated your response. Consider making it somewhat oracular (as if uttered by a sage or soothsayer). Or if a question, strangely provocative. Brevity, however, is crucial. Multivalence is preferable. *Overdetermined.*

Once the Other responds to the speech of the first actor, the first actor who is just being his or herself must take in what the Other has said. Give it a moment. Then share a true response and see where it takes you. Think about how you attribute an attitude to this Other because of what is said. You make a projection. Or you strive not to make a projection. But you take in the word of the Other all the same. What happens?

The Other makes one more attempt to hear something else and offers that to the speaker. The speaker takes it in and offers a response. At a certain point in this next response the speaker chooses simply to stop speaking and becomes the Other. That is one cycle. Now the actor who was the Other picks up the speech by truly responding to what the first actor has said and speaks of it to the other without acting. Then the first actor listens as the Other and a second cycle begins.

180   This should continue until one or both of the actors are ready to stop. If there are troubling emotions emerging at the end, the actors should work, as people, to a comfortable and acceptable close.

(That is the basic framework. Try it first as "yourself." But feel free to explore in other ways. Speak as a distinct "character" from some script or from your imagination. Speak from a "breakout" position in the Vocal Sequence.)

Because you're young, a final warning: Remember that this is ultimately an investigatory tool for expanding creativity. Goodwill is essential for this kind of exploration to be fertile. And to maintain trust. Don't play this game if you intend to be malicious. This is not a first person shooter or a chance to humiliate someone. You can provoke with your interventions, you can even be mischievous (let's say Puckish), but only because you are interested in finding new truths and new meanings which will be rewarding down the road for you and your partner.

More Fun with Talismans

Once you have completed your Talisman and compiled a list of the resulting words, you can submit the words to a variety of randomizing and poetic processes.

Look at each word in your list and try to hear other words within the words. Develop a list of such words. For instance, in the word RAVEN you might also hear RAVE and IN. In the word NOBLE you might hear NO and BULL. In TUMULT you might find TWO and MELT. The sound correspondences need not be exact. In SIZE, SIGHS. In EVADE, EVE AIDE. NOTICE, NOTE IS. ETCETERA. EGG SET ERA.

Now number the words in your two lists. Create some formula to generate number combinations such that two numbers from the original list combine with one number from the new list. Use these number combinations to link two words from the original list with one from the new. (There's no compelling reason to combine two original words with one new; choose whatever "symmetry" pleases you.) Now find an order for the three words that is most striking or meaning- ful for you, or most poetic, or evocative.

For instance, one of my sets of three words was the following: NOTICE, RAVE, FEAR. I chose to arrange them in this order: FEAR RAVE NOTICE. For me this seemed a clever way to talk about anxiety and my personal problems with the idea of success by using a "theatrical" metaphor. In other words, that which a performer should desire, a "rave notice," I might dread. For me, no other ordering of the words generated as meaningful a statement. This is the little poem that works best for me using those three words. The statement you create does not have to obey the rules of syntax. It might work for you as a name, epithet, ideograph (like a Chinese character), image, anything. I must resist offering too many more of mine as examples because some strike me as rather personal and too revealing for the world wide web (though I realize it's due in part to the private associations I make to the phrases; that's part of the fascination of this process). Well, maybe just one more--one which is rather idealistic and works as an operating principle (when not functioning as a neurotic hindrance): TUMULT IS NOBLE. And maybe one more, another fear: ART GONE COZY.

I found this to be quite an enjoyable, creatively satisfying activity (I hope not an example of "art gone cozy"). Again, one goal is to let yourself be surprised by the possible juxtapositions. Strive for the too-true-to-share. Strive to laugh in miserable recognition. Or strive to encounter the inconceivable, the personally outrageous. You are attempting, in a way, to re-double the internal echoes already reverberating from your first encounter with the original talismanic words.

Further operations are possible. List column-wise your three-word statements. Using each stacked set of two statements, box together the stacked words. For example, suppose your first two statements in your columnized list are as follows:

RANDOM EYES WISE followed by SIGHS TUMULT SOON.

The words line up and stack as follows:

RANDOM   EYES   WISE

SIGHS   TUMULT   SOON

Box together each word with its underlying word and you get three two word phrases:

RANDOM SIGHS, EYES TUMULT, WISE SOON.

How do these new phrases resonate with the history already contained in the individual words? If you wish, go further and use the three word phrases and two word phrases to create little profiles (random though they are in part), one for each of

182 the original words in your Talisman. Each word from the original Talisman appears in two two-word phrases and in two three-word. I created a visual arrangement to combine all of the phrases, the word in meaningful play through both random and determined processes. Both contingency and necessity at work?

For instance, using the original word DEATH:

DEATH / WHY

NECK / DEATH

/EAR DEATH MUSE/

/DEATH FOLD DEN/

This mini-Talisman is not meant to supplant the meanings and connections of the original; it might supplement, rather.

You can make further creative use of this material, I would hope. I am tempted to try to talk about some of this in conjunction with my discussion in the article "Work in Progress: New Performance Methods" of Lacan's mathemes (**S1, S2, $, a**) and their potential role in devising new performance strategies. Clearly, there are ways to use some of these word operations to generate new maps and territories for group performance explorations. Most importantly, of course, it's a great way to find really awesome band names. Stay tuned.

Notes for Acceptance Speech

I would like to use this opportunity to speak about Herbert Blau. Really, only Blau and his influence have brought me here today.

In my early twenties, a number of months out of college, I was on hold, biding my time, and I was lucky enough to land a job perfect for sustaining a desire to stay that way perpetually. I worked in the media library at Emory University. I could thread the projector (yes, this was a while ago) and watch *Last Year at Marienbad* during my lunch break. I lead a blessed life. I could also move through the stacks at will, reading as deeply as I wished into anything that appealed, playing *hunt the citation* in the great Gutenberg Galaxy.

I tended to juggle books that touched on the theatre with anything else emerging from that certain *French turn* in Philosophy and Criticism. I saw myself on a quest to systematically warp my perceptions in all sorts of new and interesting directions, and somehow Post-Structuralism was going to be my way to go about it. I really did think of myself as an artist looking for new answers. At that point, I was too young and cowardly to realize it was really about looking for new questions. I want to say I picked up *Blooded Though*t at some point between *Of Grammatology and Anti-Oedipus*.

To truly do justice to Blau, I know I should spend some time on his background. And on his style. And on his domain of theoretical engagement. I'm not. I am not equipped to deliver a learned and seasoned comprehensive encomium on Blau. I can report merely as one who got caught up in the writing, in that impossible vortex, and was helplessly entangled in the mystery lurking within the spin. I believe a truly seasoned academic commentator will laugh at this point because it is about to become clear that as an eager youngster in search of new highs, I fell victim to a syndrome that has afflicted many. The professional Blau scholars have watched it happen time and again to many a vulnerable and impressionable mind, have listened to an endless stream of anecdotes. That word. I beheld that word. In the middle of all the ferocious word work there appeared that one word. Here and there. In the acknowledgements and in a few of the chapters. Often popping up in the text after a nod to something characterized as a fundamental and constitutive *opacity* or as a scandalous betrayal of the whole notion of *representation* carried out by the very mimetic attempt itself or after a catalog of Heideggerian imponderables tangling and contending in a darkness beyond what can be said or seen or fleetingly grasped. The word appeared. IN ALL CAPS. I felt the dark tentacled grip of it. Always coupled with the assertion of a recollected attempt. KRAKEN.

You need to know at this point that I spent some time as a Boy Scout when I was a kid. I was not Eagle material or anything like that. I was happy and content in the rank and file. I'm not sure if I ever made it as far as First Class. I distinguished myself only once, I think I remember, by being the only member of our troop who earned the Dentistry merit badge. My mom had a cousin who taught at a dental school and so could set me up with a former student as an advisor. When left on my own, however, I lacked the initiative to soar. For me it was all about camping, the simple fun of belonging, and pouring over the Handbook with an ever-renewable fascination.

Blau referenced his work with the KRAKEN group in *Blooded Thought*, and the Boy Scout read it, eyes wide with a total readiness to align himself in any way possible. Scholars chuckle. I'm imagining they call it the KRAKEN effect: the mere word on the page acting as a prompt, as a call to some wholly indeterminate action, as a made-to-order example of Jean Laplanche's "enigmatic signifier."

The wonder of the Boy Scout Handbook lay in the setting out of ways forward for finding adventure. There were steps one could take. The only real possibility for adventure available if you think about it. There were certainly no formulas or know-how on hand for traversing the mysteries of sexuality, for instance. Nothing written down as far as that was concerned. There was no compendium one could consult to find a way forward, hence that world was destined to remain neatly divided into those who knew and those who didn't, the baffled who stood in place, and the adept who knew when to disappear around the corner. But in Scouting there was a Handbook. One could put one's desire and wonder to work. One could find answers. The Boy Scout hungrily read through *Blooded Thought* because somehow KRAKEN presented a similar set of possibilities: there was an invitation from the unknown and a suggested approach, somewhere to go and something to do, and the possibility that I wouldn't have to do it all alone, that I might be making this odd quest accepted as part of a troop.

How simple I make it all seem. Surely this is not a distinct tribute to Blau. My enthusiasm for a word on a page is not a fitting representation of the work of a great theatre artist and thinker. No, but I did not read with the mind of a scholar. I read as the Boy Scout. And I kept the Scout with me as I moved forward, undertaking a number of creative and intellectual adventures in the years to come. Often I relied on the Scout's orienteering skills, especially as I ventured into territories where I knew I lacked the proper degree of callow mental equipage to contend as a player of the first rank. When I felt my lack of layered knowingness, the Boy Scout supplied a well-timed "Golly, gee whiz" (I could sprout freckles and a pronounced Adam's apple on cue) to remind everyone I possessed the power of an un-prepossessing enthusiasm bubbling up from a non-threatening place. I was not glamorous but somehow partook of that which the ancients had in mind when naively referring to "the good" and, therefore, was acceptable as a curio.

Through a strange combination of effort and happenstance I was able to pursue my fascination with Blau and KRAKEN, the Boy Scout always at my side, always consulting the Handbook when necessary, using his imagination to speculate on a procedure when the Handbook seemed to be missing passages and pages, always ready to help find a trail that kept us safe from too much scrutiny while still moving forward.

I insisted the Boy Scout share my preoccupation with safety. You never knew when you might be called to account as you pushed along the trail. I wasn't that interested in holding forth on the flora and fauna we had passed. I could not entertain with relevant Cherokee lore about a particular stretch on a particular mountain. I had no grasp of the political climate during which such and such territory changed hands. I wanted to keep safe from revealing my lack or the non-discursive nature of my enthusiasm. Wondering if I would be able to dislocate my shoulder on cue typified the nature of my preoccupation; I didn't want to learn to hold forth on its relevance to Kierkegaard's radical turn from the Hegelian analysis of intersubjectivity. Self-protection was a priority

My concern for protection extended ultimately, of course, to hiding from Blau himself. The Boy Scout wanted to write to him, but I kept insisting we wait. It wasn't until we had walked away from the Art of the Theatre and began camping out at the University of West Georgia's Psychology Department that I gave the Boy Scout permission to send Blau a note. Blau responded warmly. He approved of the Boy Scout's unusual proposed project for earning the Self-Creation merit badge. He even gave a supportive nod to the Auto-Didactic elements on display in the attempt to bandy about the banner of Lacan and cite from a new supplement to the Handbook recently brought into the mix. I remember reading his letter as I sat at a table in the West Georgia Library. I remember my shakiness. Lacan's observation that a letter always arrives at its destination underwent an interesting variation in this instance. The letter arrived, but it did not remain. Hours after leaving the library, I discovered the letter was missing from my bag. I had left it at the library. When I had an opportunity to return there to search, it was too late. The Boy Scout grew a bit cold toward me after that.

He would still accompany me on outings and occasional overnight trips, of course. He did his best helping me navigate my clinical training, but he acknowledged that the going was getting pretty rough and the equipment was getting heavy. He began to seem less invested.

I think he understood and began to accept something long before I did. I am still trying to accept it. Each call to adventure is the beginning of a little fantasy. I bring my lunatic desire for conviction and commitment. I ask the Boy Scout to bring something simple and real to distract me, or to ground me, or to help me will the imagined into the realizable, into some play of fact that will actually mark time.

What if, when all the work is done, when the artist in me is well and truly silent, someone lifts up a log and discovers what I did, half buried there in the humus?

What if I am recognized and singled out for my contribution to the world of performance? Of letters? Of the state of the Art itself? There's the thought out of time in all of its ugly desperation, probably first churned out on a walk, the fantasy swirling into view. How to bring legitimacy to a crazy moment of hubris? The audience can't be allowed to detect the frothing at the mouth as Napoleon tries to gnaw through his straps and fight his way to the podium. I ask the Boy Scout if there's anything in the Handbook about preparing an acceptance speech. Something to provide perspective. Something modest. He's followed me up to the stage. He stands in the wings watching. He's not leafing through anything. He is not holding a compass. His arms are crossed.

He is snickering. He's about to say something. The Boy Scout can be thrifty, brave, and true, but he also is a scamp. He likes to joke. Sometimes that is his sole contribution.

(It was the Boy Scout, after all, who attempted to establish my qualifications to function as a truly knowing amanuensis to a psychology professor to whom I'd just been assigned as a graduate assistant by engaging her at the level of Critical Feminist Theory, one of her acknowledged specialties. He attached a note to the first paper she asked me to proof for her in which, amidst a few notes and suggestions, he confessed his frustration with her over-reliance on commas, suggesting to her that she had scattered them through her text like so many de-tumescent penises. This was definitely trying too hard, of course, but she did acknowledge the effort, disproving the stereotyped characterization of her ilk as wholly lacking a sense of humor. You work with what you got, or what you don't got, as the case may be. "Be prepared!" the Scout offers while grinning.)

And as I stand there waiting for some can-do guidance on an acceptance speech, the Boy Scout stifles the snickering long enough to produce: "Acceptance Speech: 'Accept. Accept. Accept. Accept.'" Okay, not that funny. Kind of dumb. But he has targeted the thing precisely. He knows how to push my buttons.

These were originally words from my mouth. It wasn't that funny when I first spoke them. I invite you to imagine at this point a Southern Dowager from generations back, still the object of ancestral worship among her family. She did her part helping establish and preserve the reach of a founding family in the smallish town in which she lived. She was characterized as a bit of a saint. The Sunday school class she taught was legend, and a book was published a few years ago that collected her writings, meditations, and teachings. You could find it at the town's locally owned bookstore. My wife's family was part of that old town mix, so we had a copy.

The title and theme touched upon acceptance. I must confess I acted like a total snot when it first came out. There was much I had yet to accept about who I was and where I was and what I was. And wasn't. So I mistreated the memory of a sweet woman, about whom I really knew very little (certainly hadn't read the book), to contend with my misery. I would sneer at my wife at opportune moments, erroneously assuming my enjoyment was shared, and intone in a voice laced with hokum: "In the words of the Dowager: 'Accept. Accept. Accept.......Accept.'"

The Acceptance Speech of a miserable creature. Really, only I have brought me here today.

I find myself entertaining the idea that the Analyst is waiting and listening for an Acceptance Speech to begin....

(The Analyst, of course, is not where I am with this malarkey. The Analyst makes a cut: *You find yourself entertaining, do you?*)

...A speech that sounds an acceptance of what, though? Where was I when I encountered the KRAKEN? I wasn't pulled under at that point, was I? Or was I myself tentatively surfacing, laced among the letters, latching on through the gaps with my own greedy tentacles? I've always been pre-occupied with orienting myself with respect to the concepts at work in the Lacanian clinic. Still clinging to the Handbook. I think maybe the Boy Scout, usually my accomplice, kicked me forward here, helping me *traverse the fantasy* on this one. I think I've manage to grasp a *drive* as well. I can grip it tightly for an instant and see it for what it is. But accept it for what I am?

Art: wince and wither

("It plumbs such depths. It subsumes so much. The question of the place and future of Art combined with a concise statement of typical male sexual response. And what of the insemination in that wince and wither? Productive? No air apparent. Wait for it. No air apparent. W(h)ence and W(h)ither. The H does not get to breath (aspirate) in this instance. No air to breed an heir. Ho Ho He He Ha Ha Much aspiration now. But what Ho He Ha do I aspire to? It's very deep, you see. Major work of Art.")

I've been assigned some occupational therapy by select concerned Mandarins of the Lichtenbergian Society. It's also something of a test, I think, to see if I can play along and get along. And be funny. It has to be funny. Even witty.

Something on Art, with the capital A. My first impulse is to send you to an earlier post in which I think I come clean on the issue of Art (introducing "The Ape"). But I can go further. Note the shape of the capital letter A. Those of you familiar with Alpine architecture will see the form of a classic high-roofed lodge. Those anthropologists among you will note the Native American "tee-pee." The capital A is clearly an icon for Shelter. Shelter is a "roof over your head" in this (upper) case. So Art is shelter; and while I seek something "over my head" to protect me from the storm, I know full well that in choosing Art for my protection: I'm in way "over my head."

In true Lichtenbergian fashion I will let this initial burst of whimsy suffice for the moment and follow it up later with the necessary elaboration (don't hold your breath). Better yet, let me be true to my belief in collaborative creative processes and open this up to a participatory fantasia. Does this particular conflicted form of Art fetish, this miserable creeping under the eaves of A, resonate for anyone else? Since your response need not be conscientious or earnest or anything in particular (we strive for Art, not accountability), do not waste time complaining you don't have enough to go on. Consider yourself provoked.

Some Guidelines for a Performance Piece

Here's an assignment from this past summer (2007). It contains a few guiding principles for composing performances that reflect, I hope, an appreciation for a wide range of experimental group efforts. Yes, ideally, a piece emerges sui generis as a response to group work and effort over time, but I wanted to articulate a few notions to nudge students out of more familiar and comfortable boxes.

Your group has just worked through a final "show" session. Using both your experiences in that session and recalling what you remember from all other performance experiences you have had with "The Sick Rose" since we began work this summer, create as a group, in about an hour-long "recapitulation" session, a Performance Piece.

Follow these Guidelines as closely as possible:

1. The piece should be brief. Five minutes could very well be two minutes too many.

2. The piece should include performance work by everyone in your group.

3. The piece should include challenging and virtuoso-level vocal and physical work.

4. The piece should involve some complex arrangement of texts, a scoring of language shared by many performers.

5. The piece must be a dense and complex encounter with your material (use a variety of materials: the original poem, research, other text, personal utterances and interpretations, realistic and abstract improvisations, memories of earlier work, etc). It should have multiple lines running simultaneously. It should be polyphonic like a Bach fugue (simultaneous presentation of many related ideas).

6. It must include difficult emotional encounters and at least one must reflect some interpersonal truth or conflict shared by two or more of the performers.

7. It must provoke questions in the viewer and a desire to view it a number of times, each time

unfolding new meanings and interpretations. It must show thoughts in action. Think of it as being more like a short provocative poem than a play, sort of like "The Sick Rose." (Note: Blake's poem The Sick Rose was the group's primary text for exploration.) Your super-objective might be to get members of the audience holding their breath; take advantage of the brevity of your piece.

8. Don't be distracted by the lures and easy pleasures of storytelling.

9. Give yourself time to view the piece a number of times in your recapitulation session so you can make additions, distill to what is most powerful, and "re-write."

10. Do not use Vocal Sequence-style repetitions of words or images or impulses unless it is vital to the piece (the repetition, remember, is foremost a route for making discoveries). Assemble your chains of action from a wide variety of work. Build slowly and thickly.

11. Use the recapitulation strategies suggest- ed by your instructor. Use others.

12. This is not a final exam. It's a different way of working. Find some joy in it. Your instructor is going to be present just to witness your process. No tips or admonishments will pass through his lips.

13. Listen to those in your group whose sensibilities might be more tuned-in to this kind of performance work. Learn from each other. Inspire one another.

Indolent. That's the last word.

Offering up this word ends the pretense. Ends the effort. Ends the need for effort. Maybe the effort was never worth it because it always seemed like a double effort or an effort folded over, already too daunting to think about. I must make an effort in order to, then, consequently, make an effort. I must make an effort in order to acquire the credible veneer of one who seems to spend his time making an effort. Even the effort I afforded this paragraph, glibly relying as it does on the repeated use of a word, was folded over, was a cover-up, an attempt to indolently get through to the end without too much effort.

I take walks most days. It's boring and meditative. I am a prisoner of the Other. I grapple with what the Other might want. Lacan 101. I offer up my thoughts. I gather up self-appraising notions. I craft aphoristic codas. I pretend I'm a wordsmith. I get the jump on time by making phrases. I stand there waiting for myself to catch up. It's all very tiring and obsessive. So, on the walk today, I proposed to the Other to offer up a word that sums it all up, that accomplishes the perfect self-evaluation. Once I proposed this, the word came fairly quickly. Indolent. I am indolent. I have always been indolent. I, baring unforeseen interventions, will always be indolent. I further told the Other that once I offered the word, I would be free of a large number of its demands. I would be off the hook.

192

And so I am. Yes, the Other will still pester me about other matters, but I now can be at peace over so many things connected with questions of energy and activity. The truth is, it's all work. And it's the kind of expenditure that is akin to treading water while trying to wave and appearing to float effortlessly. I am a treader trying to pass as a floater. And for all I know people on the shore are discussing it among themselves: *he looks so contorted trying to hide the fact he's treading; does he really think we think he's floating?* Every floater knows floating doesn't look like that. And so on.

I expect there to be some condemnation, of course. The full truth of the word *indolent* includes a certain amount of the ignoble. In other words, *indolent* is not a characterization tinged with irony. It's just true. And its despicable dimension is also true. I don't celebrate it, but I don't hide it. I am indolent. Don't expect much.

And so I can conclude at a moment's notice. I will not fret over the fact that what I have rendered here in no way sounds like the symphony of summation I unfolded during my walk. The word has freed me from that. And freed me from worrying about crafting pithy final sentences. I am now giving a last bit of effort to recalling any details from my walking meditation that I can include. I stop typing to do that now.

I resume. Why *indolent* and not *lazy*? A touch of vanity, I think. I know enough to exploit the Latin predecessors and also to see a connection with walking my own *Via Dolorosa*. Putting my occasional tears in perspective. Puffing up my pouts. Also true to my nature. *Indolent* implies that I did as a youth show some earnest effort, that I earnestly worked at my vocabulary lists. But I don't think I have ever included the word in my working vocabulary. It was kind of an accidental recall. Sure, I've read it in books. The fact that I would assure you of that is also part of my character. *Indolent* evokes for me a certain atmosphere, one in which the word *lazy* certainly has a place, but which also includes other paralyzing and paradoxical elements. And I offer that previous sentence rather than an autobiographical fantasia. Nothing to hide, just intimidated by the effort it would require to weave all of that into this.

One other thing. Maybe two further things. I have been in trance-like states of absorption in which something like creative expression has taken place.
Those moments seem, in retrospect, effortless, but they tend to be self-contained ends in themselves. No way to turn back and recapture, no way to exploit for future glory. So not part of the equation, I think. Also, I find certain distancing conventions impossible to undertake. It is very difficult to fictionalize, for instance, so that avenue is not really open to me. And maybe not really that interesting to me. Which, too, may be due to indolence. Taking upon myself the burden of others, of sharing their worlds–no energy for that. So no energy for making up lives and shouldering their cares. Abstractions have always been more amenable. Perhaps because I can pick them up and set them down without burdening myself too much. Abstractions lend themselves more easily to the trance-like improvisatory play I mentioned at the beginning of this paragraph. But, still, it's a laborious seizing of elements. Best to leave it to those who do it like breathing.

Anything further? Nope. That's it.

Writing them feels like so many dispatches issued to the Mothership. Reading them months later feels like I'm a sympathetic (and appreciative) officer on the Mothership who's thinking: from this I can tell he's learned his lesson--let's go back and pick him up.

I've kept my discussion as content-less as I possibly can.

196

Dreams of Rescue

a haiku collection

I look at my hand
dawn pale and blue through the glass
enough light to read

you could write about
the omelette   then go
out and start the car

could we go a day
and not brush the thing away
with the word **okay**

just you and the wren
even that poignant dictate
an unwelcome voice

lavender and gold
light lifts the sheet and peers in
briefly   dawn is done

cold and numb as glass
transparencies on the shelf
do not count your days

listen to the laugh
of gravel under tires and
a rooster crowing

memory of snow
new flames grow in the new chill
we could walk and walk

copper pine tine time
drop sting stand seems to soften
still stiff till step snaps

the grey road and sky
both lifted by yellow leaves
the glow of caught light

this wind's out of place
it roars its own errancy
till the exiled end

dance in rubber boots
splash puddle befuddle squish
we run from the rain

we pass dark brown groves
when did the pecan trees turn
this year we missed it

walk the morning road
the crows call   the cows moan low
feel the cold sun grow

one spine on the shelf
is a cracked and scrambled void
you must approach it

a tree spiraling
carnival light   my neighbor
strolls in a parka

the mind's cold grip on
what we call nature   we love
our adopted child

while bringing coffee
from outside a bird's bright squeak
it's a bit chilly

reduced to two tiers
two piers   at least one dipping
down while one looks out

early November
the moon casts a deep shadow
blow out the candles

look through the screen door
order sizzles in the eye
dew light on the grass

once the rain stops
the crisp echo of a finch
the chill damp black flakes

we'll crawl through this cracked
window and feed the wind forge
the cold hungry call

what is absent what
empties husks orange and red
what drives our eyes blind

morning fog brings more
more beyond more to push through
more sight more resolve

the sycamore tree
its trunk twists with history
leaves float like red smoke

sunlight breaks the lines
stipple in little notions
wait for a flutter

black licorice pines
smudge over and blot color
this is the drive home

distant mountains move
as this platinum light moves
hushed call of rain wind

are these thoughts or doubts
immobile by this brisk hum
sad to judge such things

these extremities
cold burn past the outer reach
we're all satellites

pen lines leave lambent
interstices and then bleed
out empty edges

churning trucks men with
chains a neighbor's loon-like hoots
pines spatter collapse

ecstasies occlude
the bare blue of sky is gone
these clouds shift with life

by the litter box
a damp patch renewed daily
this is how it is

grime dotes on the panes
windows write the morning cold
we consult our dreams

a few wild roses
clasp to the eye in the cold
beneath the soft veil

some morning orange
through the window a surface
reflects the sunrise

a place to see dawn
somewhere to sit and wind tight
the few first small strands

the chroma's chill sheen
eyes happy with abstraction
and remembering

laureate profile
brio gusto bravado
o mere espresso

ripe grass   feathery
tongues speak the sun   in chapel
candles for lost friends

what's left of the walk
now our air is cooling down
clouds cover like smoke

the dogs are restless
scratching licking panting hard
no sleeping for us

two decanters
on the shelf with the geisha
storage or display

time for a quick snack
there's spicy pickled okra
and chocolate milk

in the small hollow
beneath the car door handle
a tiny tree frog

absolutely still
the leaves slightly pale and dour
why this lifeless rage

peonies unfold
sleepy pink cosy blankets
moist morning air

still the theme is wind
the flicking of those branches
signs at a distance

turning a corner
a breeze assaults with autumn's
final authority

small buds shaped like pearls
throned among attendant leaves
fringes seep dark red

every year worry
is fiery transformation
underway elsewhere

Inuit envy
the vital substance   seeking
more ways to say gray

our open-toed days
squirrel with undulating tail
dog sits on her head

slowing on the curve
vast carpeting of black birds
they are not startled

pry open a place
in the phrase to hide amid
unnamed turning leaves

ornamental grass
lifting waves lining the path
to misty pastures

wearing her new shoes
today   I hope I don't look
like I'm a scene kid

lone crow on the line
we both look back behind us
the point grows too fine

the cat paws the shoe
our game's done my friend and I
stand victorious

birds scatter motifs
collect a few and fiddle
composition tip

for Fall the green leaves
exits through wee rivulets
winding through the wind

suddenly mushrooms
loose and friendly assemblies
time lost in the shade

it's September
time to wear the harvest shirt
oranges in plaid

pawing at the door
sodden heavy gray morning
the edge of the bed

she calls me over
it's time for a new tea pot
look   what do you think

cloudy arena
soon we might open windows
pull down that dead limb

thunderstorms finish
buried creek's final trickles
black fatal berries

clematis saddles
the fence to sit where the sun
touches perfectly

identifying
a certain variety
it thrives on neglect

we lift ourselves up
legs laboring on this road
breathing the morning

mother and daughter
a heart talk on the hammock
hint of summer's end

fidgeting curtains
a few bowls stacked in the sink
the radio mumbles

a drop of lemon
fogs the water in the glass
one empty doorway

a crow cries follow
willow leaves drop to the ground
sound of a black cloak

what is this tree called
shawled in the will of autumn
numb to my damp hand

moon and lamps mix beams
dreams are shadows in the yard
hard to remember

haven't walked lately
even though mornings are cool
foolish excuses

dwindling afternoon
soon this warm rainfall will end
spend or save the wait

creatures are running
cunning scampers past twigs and leaves
thieves of life and death

cold eyes of the moon
soon to see the beloved
led past where time stops

a rusted fire pit
it won't take the weight of wood
could try some pine cones

edges blurred by rain
pain of an indistinct view
new small wet patches

a moment ago
open windows found birdsong
long notes search the air

image of the dew
stewing for several days
always words away

crabapple colors
scores falling all gumball round
pounded by footsteps

which   beautiful sky
lighting up blue   when   last night
bright clouds   yes   at night

trilling canopies
leaves winking at the sidewalk
talk lost in wind gusts

morning's cold clamor
morning's flaking gold sunlight
tightening grandeur

fence is gray and white
bright repeating curlicues
views multiplying

the sun's autumn slant
antic height of ancient trees
these lanes of promise

the wind roars at will
illustrated just briefly
leaves ruffle your glance

dark open doorway
a few minutes before dawn
on the loud threshold

love is poison red
edible or not we guess
testing the berries

brief scrolls of dry bark
architecture for burning
sting of drifting smoke

would we awaken
entwined and breathing the cold
older than these woods

fog on the ball field
yields its chill to the sunshine
fine time for a walk

ladies please we need
pure sparkling crystal nostrils
to ring these high Gs

the clashing kazoos
nightly news empty pews the
blues of two by twos

we lie in ashes
morning darkens the bruises
dreams peeled unfinished

violets in my hands
the stones are stars above me
no one understands

suspended sign
the sun welcoming us west
late drive with top down

no composition
for the clouds no lines binding
the enormity

scrubby growth   the glare
of red light picking clean a
decimated barn

they charged to the far
corner and began to bark
pressed into the fence

library garden
stroll prowl a-maze-meant chase
taste glance branch delight

a hard-pressed release
of grit on the glass   little
grains of moisture

we smile   we're grateful
for the wind   a spattering
of cold and light gold

the dread in a day
that can't begin till it ends
run to the storm clouds

the green of these trees
stings tightens rings high in this
open enclosure

mimosa greetings
from that shady patch where the
way home bends and dips

air beyond balmy
new growth on the wild rose bush
sanguineous stems

the ghostly yellow
clutching of a severed vine
at the root ants swarm

blue morning glories
tasting the chilled dew   the sun
still low cool and soft

item under spring
pressure   true enough   but this
summer pressure's worse

lost in late morning
stumble through an interval
buzz of cicadas

roots displace asphalt
curled up in a warm crater
a visiting cat

dark wood a word wards
new word way through siren sounds
whose rest cue is it

moist dark soil in a
small cup on the window sill
seeds slightly covered

we are motionless
watching the fan blades inscribe
their summer circles

look at the flowers
a kindergarten marker
added this purple

no cultivation
just long years of weeds and grass
burned smooth by the sun

with the rain a past
touches   why tense against it
this soaking curtain

don't forget about
the ripening bananas
small assurances

tight-lipped growth today
nothing waiting nothing said
oaks lit from behind

insufficient light
lumps and blots about the room
it's all unfinished

a weaving young tree
a fence lattice   leaves thrown out
verdant heraldry

she turns the corner
in the museum and finds
ancient mockery

overcast blanket
as if its tight wrap is time
light burns it away

once it was their swing
this faded rope on the branch
smiling waves and walks

finally the pines
taken as companions
in the home that's here

silent and empty
a leafy proscenium
red fluttering blur

orange flame blossoms
succulent kalanchoe
it's pronounced ko-ee

slow and rollicking
branches dance in a strong wind
sharp crack of sunlight

what's outside spills in
everything's the heat of skin
scattered sunrise pinks

we're walking the tracks
grilling rails toes on the ties
quiet no noon-day freight

thumbing through the past
with a friend and then swapping
a few collectibles

tilting toward North
the light grows out of itself
a half-lidded house

rainy skies leak dawn
grey drops filling out grey thoughts
lives grabbing the keys

girls dress like gardens
butterflies and dragonflies
scruffy scratchy sun

one window view crammed
with blurred leaves   shadows arrange
that's all a face is

a want the want what
want what wants when it wants I
wants are the weak wants

why is it as it
is and what is it and why
is it what it is

rain without fanfare
wet porch damp dog heat no wind
squinting in the light

bouncing over the
fence ball lost the dog looks back
stillness and crickets

thick sky canopy
silent alabaster light
sealed and airless dome

Pink Opaque album
downloaded it   Cocteau Twins
eternal soundtrack

these bright flares of doubt
lost behind little blossoms
cool somnolent shade

a country basket
peaches soften and sweeten
shiny tomatoes

they've purple bushy
petals   gold center   hanging
from a hook drying

two empty rockers
painted a vigilant white
a motionless flag

deep bowl burnt orange
buried within the cherries
a few strawberries

two caladiums
recuperate on the stoop
many jug refills

three miles out of town
road traces of a rain storm
smell the wet static

the whole house springs up
its paws rattling   the day
is bringing something

cattle in the pond
all of them   look   all of them
she's clapping her hands

willow leaves flutter
warm currents do the plucking
morning deceptions

clay the color of
summer   scratched away layer
by layer   dry clouds

the indigo spires
threading with heat   quivering
above the nettles

says pomegranate
foetid odor now forcing
a taste   it's not bad

an owl announces
itself purposeful in this
indifferent heat

nothing but this heat
something's trying to lick me
off the planet's face

luxury of flies
of lists of windows of no
I won't or maybe

air brings all sense to
us yes two senses of sense
no air since last week

piano   tables
chairs   legs   lifting silhouettes
the glow of the floor

what seized this old elm's
imagination and swerved
its first branch skyward

come morning the cat
cries for milk   wrinkled bedrooms
no sleeping children

there's the secret glade
the word is already gone
late afternoon light

heat can't be described
instead we weigh it   I watch
my feet as I walk

temperate moments
patience to live without and
with oneself at once

in back is this one
exuberant patch of grass
leaves like eyelashes

she sends an image
tight curl stretched from edge to edge
an Atlantic wave

an absolute blot
it rolls up and weight stays it
a severe curtain

the hawk lifts and spins
its eye turning with the world
no need for a nod

dad this rain's scary
one wreck already do I
pull over and wait

wet pines glow like stone
too dark to help with waking
or with anything

as if longer days
are older and less concerned
with you and your cares

the sun stops baking
the porch around four or so
creatures gathering

this morning the sky
falls appleward clattering
with absurd song birds

love red is blood red
I guess   plenteous   but no
exotic fire reds

dandelion farming
or condemnable lawn care
it's all perspective

ivy odalisques
drowsily curled on brick steps
airless green swelter

hands behind the back
looking up   how'd the tree die
pose for a photo

sitting waiting sees
a rain puddle word searching
shimmer coruscate

obsidian stack
top heavy tilt of thunder
hope it will topple

river after rain
brown with bed mud   cat tail fleece
drifts   lights   meanders

a brief inquiry
from an old tree   abiding
tenant   your answer

hide in mother's skirt
climb up the low milky arms
child's magnolia

take the plant outside
rain will wash dust from the leaves
orioles echo

breaking formal molds
writing about our Molly
she is beautiful

drooping gerbera
its face a void in the dim
idea of a room

one nameless mountain
one bending bow of a road
light rain   grazing mare

eastern gold glistens
but senseless still lies sleeping
alongside the chill

a flowering vine
endless opportunities
its lines in longhand

rain pats andante
squeaking open the window
a cool breath descant

let's leave the sapling
one day someone will have a
spindle for their world

she intones and plucks
rhetoric and reference
cosy red berry

the air sharpened us
planing our peripheries
vital lift and drift

these ornery shrubs
won't be cubed or squared or killed
flames in a wind fight

unknown words crawl
up the fence on a green stalk
without flowering

prowl lope moan claw cry
trail tree strut hiss spit howl bite
Blues with dogs and cats

a rose abandons
will and opens everything
life and love's full end

up to the mailbox
a crow gargles in the heat
fleet snaps of crickets

a neighbor left a
paper towel wrapped bouquet
antique white roses

chipmunk's copper glint
look you never see them spring
so exposed to roads

notice our rain days
now ask us to carry more
now we dream breezes

a cadre of five
plot with double reed piping
then black wings aloft

penumbral mischief
as we pass into storm clouds
all life seen seeing

these few dandelions
dot dimensionless ether
gentle lawlessness

not on the table
not enough sun what about
here?   better?   see them?

oven hour's over
now few precious cold wishpures
what grows on the fence

her lovely moon phase
slight sliver slice cycling
a scythe for soar eyes

young holly Eye've Eve
by the bush prickly punsure
staunch this bluding harm

my comb drag kid chore
South pines rake tines needle lines
no leaf leap pay off

the garden sleeping
moonflowers   the rims of night
their hushed outpouring

this dogwood blushes
perfect motionless ardor
soft breeze on my neck

a delicate bird
wriggles through dust stones and straw
then hops up and off

kneeling from the trunk
bearing a bowl of milk   one
tiny apple tree

open every door
and window no out no in
all wind all shadows

sight suddenly tugged
by the Japanese maple
red velvety depths

will she notice the
first emerging bud and say
look   a knock-out rose

we're slapped by wet leaves
mute hues green and black with dew
the weight of chilled breath

lots of talk of lots
ribbon to ribbon we walked
inexplicable

let's walk down our street
turning toward that tangled stretch
to see the bamboo

we get used to things
fresh flowers on the table
cat on the table

soggy indigo
clouds in retreat   dusk glows gold
long scratches of trees

red camellias
their buoyant dance on storm winds
sturdier than hearts

wild azalea
blooms brought inside very soon
close like umbrellas

blue   full and empty
half the time   sky seems alive
where else can I look

wounded petals lost
but delirious storm winds
find another truth

yesterday the chill
left too soon   all dislodged soil
dried   faded to dust

our shepherd barks
a dogwood limb floats in frame
so many birdsongs

over the rise sheared
planes of sun drop through ice clouds
rotund leafed giants

the path still shadowed
fragrance of wisteria
tender choke of vines

something seeks to use
troublesome tenses   stealing
precious syllables

leaves ask for patience
each an open upright hand
a long wait for figs

the roots of this pine
feeding close to the surface
still make us stumble

stay like this   damp   cool
the sky's wide metallic sheen
wet curling leaves   wind

storm's piecemeal advance
higher partials of birdsong
flashing messages

nothing good to say
about blue jays seeing two
recalling Dad's view

these azaleas
miss the first hoopla of Spring
we wait for purple

the sound of dispute
cold winds shoulder resistance
to the growing warmth

this morning's limit
my unsheltered shivering
lunatic vigil

each raindrop seizes
a small blossom to witness
its dissolution

this sky should be shared
this ancient pewter tankard
full of rainwater

a few splotches of green
on the bank three cardinals
poised and attentive

what would more names do
for these scattered clouds   a moth
settles on my shirt

a broad costly arc
the pine branch dips with treasure
cradling tight green cones

the wooded hillside
not yet obscured by the Spring
our pact still exposed

tracks run alongside
barbed wire woven with wild shrubs
beyond that   pastures

young leaves are dying
from a snap frost   they roar red
before this late sunlight

a squirrel flickering
somewhere its world assembled
in bits   word by word

during her breakfast
she pauses and turns to me
she likes hearing birds

momentary slant
late sun touching sycamores
an old lane invites

blossoms have fallen
the tulip tree spreads its skirt
moist and sorrowful

two egrets leaving
early sun and endless grass
its green translucence

marsh soil is slate grey
bright grains   then the infusion
of brine and blackness

Sapelo marshes
would we ever beg for love
with abject fragrance

pines grip a red slope
dry suckle of memory
the heat has odor

clouds on the skyline
drain shadows   unexpected
small purple flowers

let the tailored rows
of pear tree blossoms approach
reckless galaxies

before dawn the moon
or some dream of a blue sun
a chill on our arms

an old horse   gold as
the winter meadow   submits
tethered to our glance

immobilizing
faintness of this morning's light
three dogs on the bed

perhaps fat with eggs
a wren bounces on the sill
shattering the view

this warming sunlight
slender trunk of silver   Spring's
deep crimson seepage

old ivy wrapped tree
it's branches claw   no   I claw
through venous rapture

a grey barn unrolls
triangular weathered grand
I should stop but don't

barely swollen buds
draw the falling flakes   they cling
the branch tips twinkle

children on the slope
snow still falls   a thick silent
shower white as cream

frost light has a sound
a bright squeak   a bird somewhere
just one   unanswered

rain mutters under
thunder   the sky unfolding
dim light for reading

precisely as I
turn the pine branch twists deforms
thrilling flirtation

an ugly hope here
crepe myrtles lopped to their trunks
they had grown too full

beyond the treeline
dampness broods   our last fire's ash
spread around rose thorns

trees clutching grey sheets
loyal enemy of spring
the cold wish of wind

some days a garden
would be nice   fence with ivy
a low place to sit

rabbits spaniels saints
concrete casts   shadowy stains
of life   black and green

momentary light
realigns a room   golden
orb of the morning

can you see them there `
by that old damp shovel's blade
the early onions

the hushed din of birds
embellishing the legend
bards of last night's storms

a creek's adventure
through the ravine scramble down
toss in a pale leaf

the thing to notice
first is the empty hammock
then the empty oaks

a sleeping turn to
the light   blind lifted   cats know
no interruptions

a fire warms the late
afternoon light   a dog tries
the wine and walks off

in here everything's
in piles   something's wrong with that
dogs trot back and forth

you know the window
is half open   dawn's cold air
thick with memory

black sky   a bare elm
two crows on top   then three   then
four announcing rain

nothing close to green
in view through windows   through thoughts
a vast gleaming grey

cats leave the willow
infinite delicacy
down the spiral steps

at dusk black branches
pulse   life pushes towards us
close an eye   it stills

somewhere above geese
offer stippled chattering
whippoorwills answer

incendiary
an oddly cold word today
this frost-free morning

a single teabag
dangles in the holly bush
still damp and heavy

leaves screening the light
and at work in each warm cell
a dream of rescue

Marc Honea has spent time working in public mental health and in the theatre, two vanishing entities. Or one and the same vanishing entity. He resides with his family in Newnan, Georgia.

www.ingramcontent.com/pod-product-compliance
Lightning Source LLC
Chambersburg PA
CBHW062037090426
42740CB00016B/2938